NEVER GET BORED BOOK

Written by James Maclaine,
Sarah Hull and Lara Bryan

Illustrated by Jacob Souva, Ellie O'Shea,
Kyle Reed and Briony May Smith

Designed by Stephen Moncrieff, Katie Webb,
Melissa Gandhi and Sarah Vince

BORED, HUH?

Then, give these boredom-busting techniques a try.

1

Describe how bored you are in an inventive way.

For instance...

I'm as bored as an astronaut floating in a spacecraft, who hasn't spoken to anyone for 1,001 days, and can't even see out of the window because it's misted over.

Can you do better?

2

Rearrange the letters in I'M SO VERY BORED, to make as many different words as you can.

dire

Rome

robed

Can you make ten new words?

3 Try saying 'I'm bored' as quickly...

...then as slowly as possible.

How many times can you say 'I'm bored' in ten seconds?

4 Write the word BORED in as many different styles as you can. You could use these ideas:

BORED   BORED
BORED   Bored
Bored   BORED

And that was only to get you started!

5 Or how about memorizing words for 'bored' in twelve different languages?

gelangweilt (German)	bosan (Malay)	diflasu (Welsh)
verveeld (Afrikaans)	kyllästynyt (Finnish)	aburrido (Spanish)
entediado (Portuguese)	annoiato (Italian)	znuděný (Czech)
chán (Vietnamese)	nababato (Filipino)	ennuyé (French)

You'll discover lots more ideas throughout this book.

Just flip through its pages, open the book at random, or browse the contents on pages 4–5.

Some of the things in this book have answers or solutions. You can find all of these on pages 126–127.

INSTEAD OF GETTING BORED...

These words are in Latin. Turn to pages 78-79 to find out why...

For drawing tips, look
at pages 6-7,
48-49 and 94-95.

Elephants have their
own 'language'!
See page 102.

PICK UP A PENCIL

Find some paper and take a line for a walk.

Try to keep your pencil on the page at all times!

Try out straight lines.

loop the loop.

Go up, down, up, down...

Use your pencil on its side.

Zigzag down the page.

Press down really hard.

What will you draw?

COPY CAT

Copy this monster onto a piece of paper.

AGAINST THE CLOCK

Try to draw it again, but only give yourself one minute to do so.

DON'T LOOK DOWN

This time, keep looking at the monster as you draw. Don't look at the page you're drawing on.

DON'T PEEK

Now, close the book. Draw the monster on a new piece of paper from memory.

Draw the monster again with the hand you don't usually use.

TEST YOUR SENSES

You use your senses all the time, but can you always trust what you smell, taste, feel, see or hear?

Taste test

Carefully cut a small piece of onion and a small piece of apple, then wash your hands. Pinch your nose between your finger and thumb and taste one then the other.

Is it hard to tell the difference? That's because most of what you taste actually comes from your sense of smell.

Tricky touch

Roll a small ball of poster tack around on a table with your fingers crossed and eyes closed.

Does it feel as if you're rolling two balls? As the ball touches the outside of both fingers your brain thinks that there are two balls.

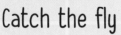

Catch the fly

Play this game with a friend somewhere quiet, to test your sense of hearing.

One player, the 'fly', softly rubs their thumb and index finger together, while moving this hand around. The other person, with eyes closed, listens for the 'fly' and tries to grab the finger and thumb.

Spot it

Can you spot two Ns in this sea of Ms?

MMMMMMMMMMMMM
MMMMMMMMMMMMMM
MMMMMMMMMMMMMM
MMMMMMMMMMMMMNMM
MMMMMMMMMMMMMM
MMMMMMMMMMMMMM
MMMMMMMMMMMMMM
MMMMMMMMMMMMMM
MMMNMMMMMMMMMM
MMMMMMMMMMMMMM
MMMMMMMMMMMMMM

Because M and N look similar, and most of the letters in this grid are Ms, your brain assumes that they're *all* Ms.

Keep exploring your senses

TWEET **TWEET**

1
Pat your tongue dry with a paper towel and put some sugar on your tongue. Does it taste less sweet than you expect?

That's because chemicals in food need to dissolve in saliva in your mouth for you to taste things properly.

2
Make a list of ten smells you like and ten smells you loathe.

Scientists estimate that most people can detect around 1,000,000,000,000 different smells. That's one trillion!

3
Sit by an open window and write down how many sounds you can hear. Then close your eyes and listen again. Can you hear more things?

You can tune in better to your sense of hearing if you take away your sense of sight.

DISCOVER EXTRA SENSES, TOO...

Balance

Try spinning around ten times. Do you feel dizzy, even after you stop?

Yes. This is because fluid in your ear, which helps you to balance, keeps on spinning after you stop – so your brain thinks you're still moving.

Proprioception

Can you close your eyes and touch your nose?

YES

Even with your eyes closed, you know exactly where your nose is. This awareness of your body is called proprioception.

Synesthesia

Try listening to a song and doodling on a piece of paper at the same time. Does the music inspire you to use certain shades of pens or draw any particular shapes or patterns?

A few people really can *see* sounds, *taste* shapes and *smell* words. This ability, where several senses blend together to create a new kind of perception, is called synesthesia.

STAGE A SHADOW PUPPET SHOW

Impress your audience by making all these different animal shadow shapes with your hands.

Wait until it's dark, then shine a spotlight on a wall. Switch off all the other lights in the room.

Hold your hands in front of the light to cast shadows onto the wall.

This bird appears to fly when you flap your hands.

Wiggle your fingers, so the rabbit's ears twitch.

Make a dog appear to bark. Just open and close your little fingers.

Flick your fingers to bend an elephant's trunk.

Snap your hands – or a crocodile's jaws – together.

Two narrow strips of paper between your fingers make a snake's tongue.

Make a fist for a **snail's** shell.

Use the fingers on your left hand for **deer** antlers.

NOW... add SCENERY

Cut out shapes from thick paper.

Attach them to straws with tape.

Ask someone to hold them in front of the light to make more shadow shapes.

Shadow play

Some shadow puppeteers use intricate, cut-out figures for puppets, with moveable body parts. According to a Chinese legend, the first such puppet was made over 2,100 years ago when...

Emperor Wu was overcome with grief. Li, the woman he loved was dead.

If only someone could bring her back to life.

Hearing the Emperor's pleas, a magician named Shao Weng made a likeness of Li out of leather and dressed it in her clothes.

Shao Weng hid inside a torchlit tent, ready to perform.

And when darkness fell, Emperor Wu was amazed to see what looked like Li's shadow move again.

AIM PAPER PLANES

FIRST make a plane...

1 Fold a rectangular piece of paper in half.

2 Fold up the bottom right corner to the middle.

3 Fold this flap over to the middle again.

4 Fold it one last time.

5 Turn the piece of paper over.

6 Repeat steps 2 to 4 on this side.

1 Open up the wings. Your plane is ready to fly.

THEN make targets...

1 Join two sheets of newspaper together with tape.

2 Draw around plates or bowls of different sizes and cut out circles.

3 Hang the holey newspaper from the top of a doorframe with two pieces of sticky tape.

To launch your plane, hold it just in front of the middle, and throw.

THE
FIRST FLYERS

Over 100 years ago, brothers Orville and Wilbur Wright invented the first plane that could take off and land under its own power.

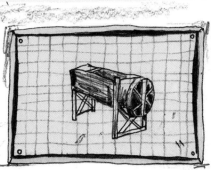

The brothers tested different wing designs in a purpose-built wind tunnel...

EUREKA!

...until they found the best one.

It took another six weeks for their mechanic Charlie Taylor to build an engine. Then, the *Wright Flyer* was ready to fly.

Wilbur and Orville tossed a coin to see who would pilot it.

And on the morning of December 17, 1903, at 10:35...

...it was Orville who made the first successful flight. It lasted just 12 seconds covering a distance of 36.6m (120ft).

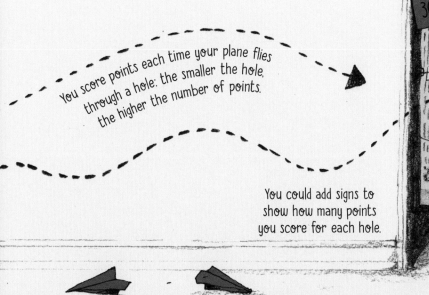

You score points each time your plane flies through a hole: the smaller the hole, the higher the number of points.

You could add signs to show how many points you score for each hole.

DISCOVER ACCIDENTAL INVENTIONS

Follow the lines to read the strange stories behind some inventions.

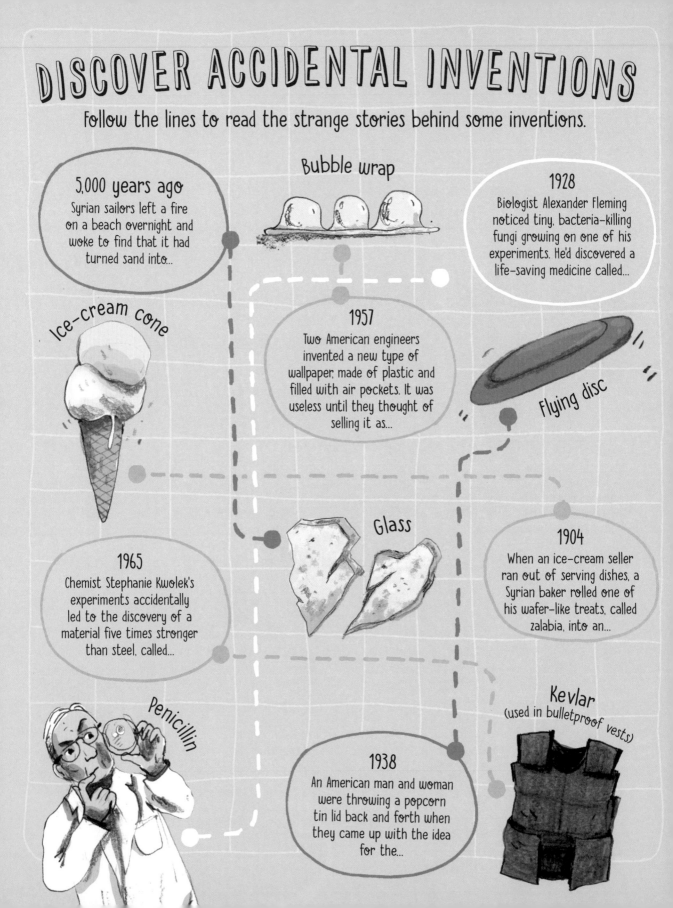

5,000 years ago
Syrian sailors left a fire on a beach overnight and woke to find that it had turned sand into...

Bubble wrap

1928
Biologist Alexander Fleming noticed tiny, bacteria-killing fungi growing on one of his experiments. He'd discovered a life-saving medicine called...

Ice-cream cone

1957
Two American engineers invented a new type of wallpaper, made of plastic and filled with air pockets. It was useless until they thought of selling it as...

Flying disc

Glass

1965
Chemist Stephanie Kwolek's experiments accidentally led to the discovery of a material five times stronger than steel, called...

1904
When an ice-cream seller ran out of serving dishes, a Syrian baker rolled one of his wafer-like treats, called zalabia, into an...

Kevlar
(used in bulletproof vests)

Penicillin

1938
An American man and woman were throwing a popcorn tin lid back and forth when they came up with the idea for the...

WILD INVENTIONS

In 1997, Japanese engineers copied the streamlined shape of kingfishers' beaks to design ultra-fast bullet trains.

Geckos have thousands of tiny hairs on their toes. They help them climb up walls.

Can you think of any new inventions that geckos and sharks could inspire?

Shark skin is made of tiny, tooth-shaped scales, so ocean gunk can't stick to it.

NOW... make a gloopy substance.

YOU WILL NEED:

half a small glass of cornflour (cornstarch)

a quarter of a glass of cold water

a few drops of food dye in any shade

1 Stir everything together in a bowl.

2 Then, use your hands to make a sticky gloop.

What will you call your gloopy creation?

MAKE MUSIC

Build and play four different musical instruments.

Shoebox guitar

You will need:
a pencil
a mug
an old shoe box
scissors
6 rubber bands
tape

1
Draw around a mug on the lid of a shoe box. Push a pencil through the line you've drawn to make a hole. Then, cut out the circle through this hole.

2
Fold up the left and right 'sides' of the circle, to make a 'bridge'. Stick it on the lid with tape, next to the hole.

3
Put the lid on the shoe box. Stretch six long rubber bands around the box, over the hole and bridge.

4
Pluck and strum the rubber bands. You can make a higher note by pressing your finger down on a rubber band while you pluck it.

Top view

Hole

This is the bridge.

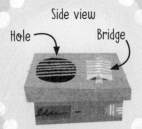

Side view

Hole   Bridge

Do thick rubber bands make different sounds from thin ones?

Pan drum

Cover a saucepan
with a piece of baking parchment.
Secure it with a large rubber band
to make a drum.

Use a wooden spoon
for a drum stick.

Bottle maracas

Put some rice, lentils or dried
beans in two plastic bottles.

Screw on the lids
and shake together.

Glass xylophone

Fill six glasses with different amounts
of water. Line them up in height order.

Tap each glass with a
metal spoon. Which one
makes the lowest note?

Form a BAND!
Play your instruments
in a group.

17

STRETCH YOUR BRAIN

Bird's eye view

What does each of these pictures show? They're all seen from above.

Say what you read

Read out the names of the animals on the left, then try to do the same with the ones on the right...

lion
crocodile
giraffe
zebra
hippo
meerkat
elephant
rhino

zebra
meerkat
hippo
rhino
crocodile
elephant
giraffe
lion

It's harder, isn't it?

Turn around

These lines are in the shape of a donkey. Can you think how to make it face the other way by moving just one of the lines?

Once you know the answer, you could make the above shape using straws, pens or pencils, and challenge others to turn it around too.

Conundrum

What can you hold in your left hand but not in your right?

Read this...

These words are written in mirror writing. Italian artist and inventor Leonardo da Vinci often wrote this way – but no one knows why. It is much easier to read if you look at the words in a mirror.

After shot

What do you think happened just before this scene?

Riddles of the Sphinx

I'm a sphinx. According to Ancient Greek stories, I eat anyone who can't solve my riddles. Do you dare to try to answer these ones?

1
What has two heads, four eyes, six legs and a trunk?

2
What begins with an 'e' and ends with an 'e', but only has one letter in it?

3
What two things can you never have for breakfast?

19

JUGGLE

You'll need three balls, plenty of space and patience.

1 ball

Throw a ball back and forth, from one hand to the other, making an even arch shape.

Try to throw the ball so it's level with your eyes when it reaches the top of the 'arch'.

As you catch the ball, move your hand a little closer to your other hand in a small curve and throw it again.

Try doing it without looking at the ball, and then with your eyes closed.

2 balls

Start with one ball in each hand.

Throw ball 1 in an arch shape.

When it reaches the top of the arch...

...throw ball 2, and catch ball 1.

Then, catch ball 2 with your other hand.

Repeat this step until you can do it without looking at the balls. Then try swapping hands, so you start with your other hand, too.

3 balls

Start with two balls in one hand, and one ball in the other.

Throw ball 1 in an arch shape.

As ball 1 reaches the top of the arch...

...throw ball 2, and catch ball 1.

As ball 2 reaches the top of the arch...

...throw ball 3, and catch ball 2.

Then, catch ball 3.

Once you can do this without dropping any balls, keep throwing and catching in the same pattern. It'll take lots of practice.

TIE KNOTS

Try tying these knots with some rope or string.

Pull

Pull

Overhand knot

Figure-eight knot

Square knot – for tying two ropes together

A magician named Harry Houdini (1874–1926) taught himself how to tie and untie knots with his toes.

Sling knot – for carrying a bucket that's missing its handle

Place rope under bucket.

Tie a loop over the top like this.

Pull loop apart and slip it over rim of bucket.

Tighten loop around bucket.

Knot together ends of rope to make a handle.

COLLECT STAMPS

Remove stamps from old envelopes and keep them in a notebook or album.

1 Cut around a stamp that's stuck to an envelope. Place it in a bowl of warm water.

2 After ten minutes, the stamp should have come away from the envelope. If not, peel it off carefully.

3 Leave the stamp on a piece of paper towel to dry. Then, stick it in your album – use glue or 'stamp mounts' that you can buy online.

You can buy bundles of old stamps online to add to your collection.

Arrange the stamps in your album by date, country of origin or type.

Ask people you know to save any envelopes with stamps for you.

STAMP TRIVIA

Stamp collecting is known as philately.

In 2013, stamps that smelled and tasted like chocolate were made in Belgium.

Only one British Guiana 1c magenta stamp from 1856 is known to exist. It sold for $9,480,000 in 2014, making it the world's most valuable stamp.

Write about a haunted house

Imagine you've just walked through the front door into the haunted house below. Write about your visit using the lists of words and story prompts to help you. Start at the entrance gates...

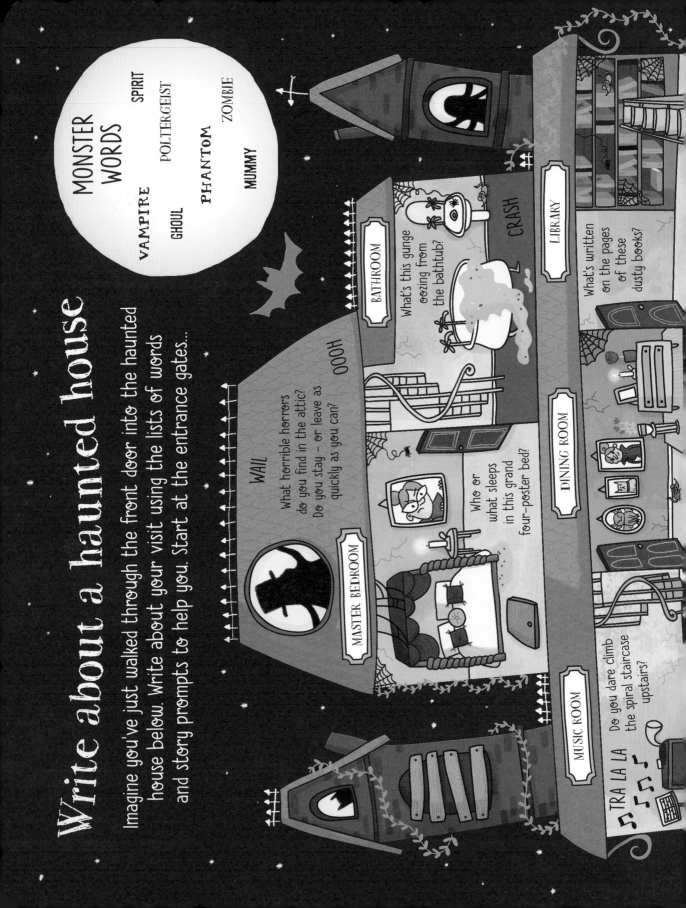

MONSTER WORDS

SPIRIT

POLTERGEIST

ZOMBIE

VAMPIRE

PHANTOM

GHOUL

MUMMY

BATHROOM

What's this gunge oozing from the bathtub?

CRASH

LIBRARY

What's written on the pages of these dusty books?

OOOH

WAIL

What horrible horrors do you find in the attic? Do you stay – or leave as quickly as you can?

MASTER BEDROOM

Who or what sleeps in this grand four-poster bed?

DINING ROOM

TRA LA LA Do you dare climb the spiral staircase upstairs?

MUSIC ROOM

Open the trap door at the top of the stairs.

KITCHEN

What's that strange smell wafting from the stove?

What's bubbling in the cauldron?

SPOOKY WORDS

PITCH-BLACK SCREECHING CLOTTED
LOOMING WHISPERING SHRIEK
SLAMMED DREADFUL DEADLY
FLITTING HIDEOUS EERIE
EAR-SPLITTING ECHOED GLOOPY

What kind of frightful food is being served up for dinner?

What tune is playing on the piano?

ENTRANCE HALL

Can you hear any noises coming from upstairs?

Who are the people in these creepy portraits?

CREAK CREAK CREAK

ENTER at YOUR oWn riSK!

HERE LIES FRED (buried alive).

RIP Rascal the Rabbit

START

TELL YOUR FORTUNE

Make a folded 'fortune teller' to find out your future.
You'll need a square piece of paper. There are instructions for turning
a rectangular piece of paper into a square on page 90.

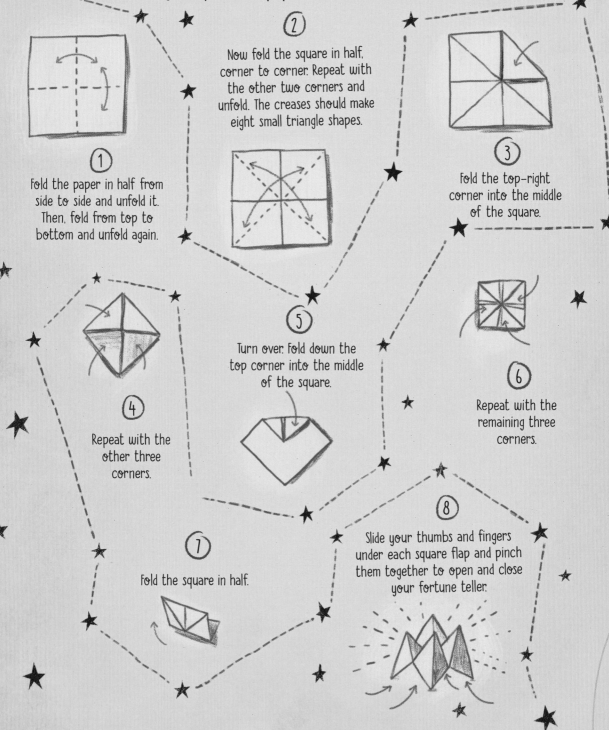

②

Now fold the square in half,
corner to corner. Repeat with
the other two corners and
unfold. The creases should make
eight small triangle shapes.

①

Fold the paper in half from
side to side and unfold it.
Then, fold from top to
bottom and unfold again.

③

Fold the top-right
corner into the middle
of the square.

⑤

Turn over. Fold down the
top corner into the middle
of the square.

④

Repeat with the
other three
corners.

⑥

Repeat with the
remaining three
corners.

⑦

Fold the square in half.

⑧

Slide your thumbs and fingers
under each square flap and pinch
them together to open and close
your fortune teller.

FILL IT OUT

Unfold your fortune teller and fill it out using the creases as guides. Then, turn it over so the blank side is facing up and fold again following the steps on the previous page.

Draw a spot in each corner using four different shaded pens.

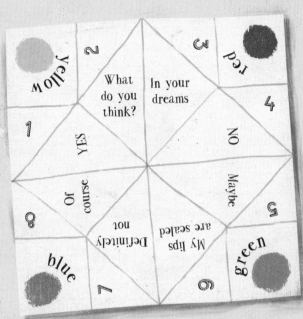

Write eight messages in the large triangles. These are answers to questions you will ask the fortune teller (see below). Make up your own or use these suggestions.

Write the numbers 1 to 8 in the triangles either side of the corners.

The fortune teller text (as shown in image):
- yellow — 2
- red — 3
- 4
- 1
- What do you think?
- In your dreams
- YES
- NO
- Of course
- Maybe
- 8
- blue — 7
- Definitely not
- My lips are sealed
- green — 6
- 5

HOW TO PLAY

2 Pick one of the spots. Spell the word aloud, opening and closing your fortune teller alternate ways for each letter.

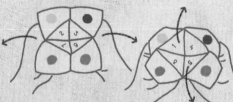

1 Ask any question you like. For instance...

Will I save the world?

Can I pass the test?

For instance, if you choose the blue spot, you open and close the fortune teller four times.

3 Choose a number from the four you can see inside. Open and close the fortune teller alternate ways this many times.

4 Pick another number. Open up that flap and read the answer to your question.

BECOME A PASTA COGNOSCENTE*

*Cognoscente is an Italian word for someone who knows a lot about a particular subject.

Italian pasta comes in hundreds of different shapes. How many do you know?

Fusilli means 'little springs'. It's the most popular pasta.

Radiatori look like old-fashioned radiators.

Farfalle is Italian for 'butterflies'.

Strozzapreti translates as 'priest-stranglers'.

This shape is named after quill pens, or **penne**, because its ends are also slanted.

These pasta shapes are **creste di galli**. They resemble the combs that grow on male chickens' heads.

Ravioli are squares of stuffed pasta. The name means 'little turnips'.

TURN LEFTOVERS INTO TORTA DI PASTA

(Italian for pasta cake)

2 large mugs of cooked pasta

2/3 of a mug of milk

1 mug of cherry tomatoes, halved

2 handfuls of fresh spinach

1 mug of hard cheese, grated

pepper

two eggs

Make layers of pasta, spinach, tomato and cheese in an ovenproof dish.

Stir the egg, milk and a few grindings of pepper together with a fork. Pour over the top.

Bake for 25 minutes at 180°C (360°F), or until the cheese on top is crispy.

For extra crunch, sprinkle bread crumbs on top!

NOW TRY... eating spaghetti like an Italian.

Italians use a fork to eat spaghetti, and they NEVER cut it into pieces.

Spaghetti means 'little strings'.

1
Pick out one or two strands of spaghetti with your fork and lift the fork to separate them.

2
Put your fork prongs down on the side of your plate and twirl the fork clockwise to wind up the spaghetti.

3
Lift the fork to your mouth and pop the spaghetti in.

The longest piece of spaghetti ever made was 3,776m (over 2.3 miles) long.

PASTA PUZZLES

If you pulled both ends of these spaghetti tangles, which of them would tie a knot?

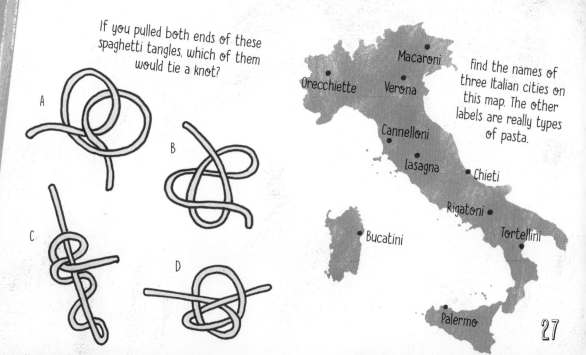

A

B

C

D

Find the names of three Italian cities on this map. The other labels are really types of pasta.

Macaroni

Orecchiette

Verona

Cannelloni

Lasagna

Chieti

Rigatoni

Tortellini

Bucatini

Palermo

If you haven't got any dice, here's how to make one. You can use it to play the games on the opposite page, and on pages 36–37 and 68–69.

1. Put a piece of tracing paper or baking parchment over this template. Use a ruler and pencil to draw over the lines.

2. Turn over the tracing paper or parchment and put it on a piece of thick paper. Draw over your lines pressing hard.

3. The pencil lines should now show on the thick paper. Cut around the outside of the template on the thick paper.

4. Write the numbers 1 to 6 on the sides.

5. Fold along the lines to make a cube shape. The flaps (the yellow parts on the template) can be tucked inside.

6. Put glue on the flaps and stick them inside the cube.

Template numbers: 3, 5, 6, 2, 4, 1

Get to 100

Throw a dice five times. Write down the number it shows each time. Can you make 100 – or another big number of your choice – by adding, subtracting and multiplying together the numbers you threw?

$$5 \times 4 = 20$$
$$6 - 1 = 5$$
$$20 + 5 = 25$$
$$25 \times 4 = 100$$

Cat's whiskers

Players take turns rolling a dice and drawing their own pictures of a cat, one part at a time.

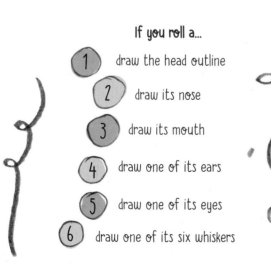

If you roll a...

1 — draw the head outline

2 — draw its nose

3 — draw its mouth

4 — draw one of its ears

5 — draw one of its eyes

6 — draw one of its six whiskers

You must draw the head first. So you need to throw a 1 to start.

Then you can draw the other parts in any order.

The WINNER is the first person to complete a cat picture.

SURVIVE IN THE JUNGLE

Imagine you're a jungle explorer and discover some survival techniques for your expedition...

The rest of your team has gone ahead, but they left this pattern of twigs for you to follow. Use the key to track them on the map.

START

SURVIVAL TIP #1

To find water, head downhill.

If you can't find any, dig a hole. There might be some underground.

KEY

↑	Go straight ahead
→	Take first right
←	Take first left
⫢→	Go over obstacle then right
←⫢	Go over obstacle then left
⋀⋀⋀⋀	Cross water

SURVIVAL TIP #2

If you see a snake, back off slowly – most snakes will be eager to escape.

SURVIVAL TIP #3

If you need to cross a fast-flowing river, use a stick to help you balance.

And shuffle across sideways.

DINNER TIME

Insects are a handy source of food in the jungle. Use the chart below to identify which of these bugs you could eat if you were desperate and which you should leave alone.

A

B

C

D

E

F

G

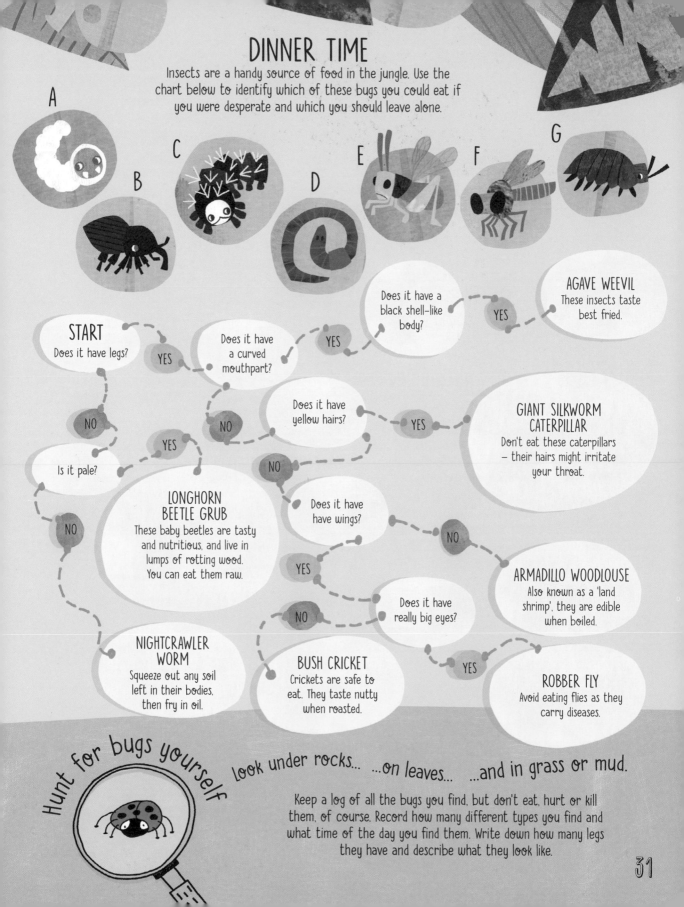

AGAVE WEEVIL
These insects taste best fried.

START
Does it have legs?

YES

Does it have a curved mouthpart?

YES

Does it have a black shell-like body?

YES

NO

NO

NO

YES

Is it pale?

YES

Does it have yellow hairs?

YES

GIANT SILKWORM CATERPILLAR
Don't eat these caterpillars – their hairs might irritate your throat.

NO

LONGHORN BEETLE GRUB
These baby beetles are tasty and nutritious, and live in lumps of rotting wood. You can eat them raw.

Does it have have wings?

NO

NO

ARMADILLO WOODLOUSE
Also known as a 'land shrimp', they are edible when boiled.

YES

Does it have really big eyes?

NIGHTCRAWLER WORM
Squeeze out any soil left in their bodies, then fry in oil.

NO

BUSH CRICKET
Crickets are safe to eat. They taste nutty when roasted.

YES

ROBBER FLY
Avoid eating flies as they carry diseases.

Hunt for bugs yourself

look under rocks... ...on leaves... ...and in grass or mud.

Keep a log of all the bugs you find, but don't eat, hurt or kill them, of course. Record how many different types you find and what time of the day you find them. Write down how many legs they have and describe what they look like.

31

LEARN TO BEATBOX

Beatboxers use three basic sounds.
Each one is named after a different part of a drum kit.

HI-HAT 'TS'

Close your teeth, bring your tongue forward and make a 'Ts' sound.

SNARE DRUM 'KA'

Make a snare sound by holding your breath and releasing the air as you pronounce the 'Ka'.

BASS DRUM 'PUH'

Hold your breath and make a loud 'Puh' sound. The more it sounds like blowing a raspberry, the better.

Musicians started beatboxing in the 1980s in New York. They mimicked the sounds made by expensive drum machines, known as 'beat boxes'.

Now try making all the sounds in a sequence:

PUH TS KA TS | PUH TS KA TS...

You can vary the rhythm by inserting two fast hi-hat sounds.

PUH TS TS KA TS | PUH TS TS KA TS...

Try inserting a pause "–" between sounds.

PUH TS KA TS | - TS KA -...

Make your own sequence of sounds. Write them down to help you perform.

GO BANG!

You need to use old gift wrap or newspaper.

Did you know that you can make a surprisingly loud noise with a large rectangular sheet of thin paper? Here's how...

1 Fold the longest sides of the paper together and then unfold them.

2 Fold each corner into the middle crease.

3 Fold the paper in half along the middle crease, from bottom to top.

4 Now fold in half from right to left, and unfold again.

5 Fold up both bottom corners so that the bottom edges meet in the middle crease.

6 Turn the paper over and fold it in half from left to right.

NOW...
Hold the paper at the open end with the long edge facing you.

Raise your hand in the air and flick it down very sharply.

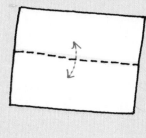

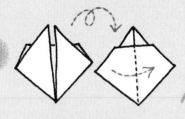

BANG

THE
LOUDEST BANG
IN HISTORY

On August 27, 1883, the volcanic island of Krakatoa, in Indonesia, exploded, making the loudest sound ever recorded.

People could hear the explosion as far as 3,000 miles away.

MASTER PHOTO TRICKS

If you have a camera or smart phone, you don't need fancy equipment to create special effects. Just try the techniques on these two pages.

Cliffhanger

1 Ask someone to lie on the floor and pretend to 'climb'. Crouch down and take a photo.

2 Rotate the photo on screen so it is upside down, or print it out, to do the same.

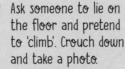

Fun with filters

Shady shots

If you take a photo through one of the lenses in a pair of sunglasses, you'll get a tinted picture.

Googly eyes

To get googly eyes, fill a glass with water. Hold it in front of one eye, and take a selfie.

fantastic frame

Take framed portraits of people using this trick...

1 Draw a frame on a large piece of very thick paper. Carefully cut it out.

2 Stick two straws or pencils on the back of the frame with tape.

3 Ask your subject to hold up the frame. Then take a photograph.

You could cut around the edges of the frame after printing the photo.

Surprising close-ups

Make ordinary things look extraordinary by taking close-up photos.
Can you guess what these photos really show?

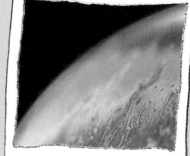

1. Undiscovered planet?

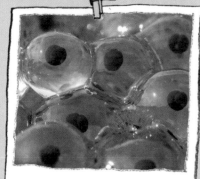

2. Alien eyes?

3. Dragon skin?

NOW TRY THIS...

Make your own close-up quiz.
Take photos and give them misleading titles.

PLAY ROAD RACE

This is a game for two players on a car or bus journey. But you can play it anywhere you like with a dice.

FINISH

Hold the book between you.

Touch the start square on your side of the book with your finger.

Each time you see a car out of the window that's a similar shade to one on the board, move your finger to the next orange or purple spot.

Wait with your finger there until you see another matching car.

Keep moving in the direction of the cars on the board.

The first player to reach the finish line is the winner.

START

FINISH

START

37

SOLVE MYSTERIES

Wednesday, March 15

No. 32,751

Think you're the next Sherlock Holmes? Then read this newspaper and deduce explanations for the four unsolved crimes.

PROBLEM POISONING

Detectives remain baffled after the curious death of Lord Livingstone and the even curiouser survival of his wife Lady Lavinia at their country home.

Toxicology reports confirmed that death by strychnine poisoning occurred after the couple drank lemonade.

Lady Lavinia said: "I just don't understand it. Bertie (Lord Livingstone) only drank the one glass... I was so thirsty that I polished off the rest. Surely it's me who should be dead?"

The case continues.

Above: Lord and Lady Livingstone, shortly before the former's demise

THE VANISHING VANDAL

Investigations into the recent destruction of a priceless Ming vase at the Museum of Fine Art have stalled. Readers may recall that the vase was found smashed to smithereens on the morning of March 4th.

The museum had been locked overnight and although a

Above: The vase before disaster struck

window had been left open, the grille across it meant no one could have entered.

A gunshot was heard around 3am, but no bullet was found on the scene. There was, however, a tiny puddle of water next to the broken vase, for which no explanation has been found.

WHODUNNIT? GETAWAY CAR GETS AWAY

A fourth man was arrested last night in connection with the abduction of prize-winning racehorse Clanstar.

A thief broke into Springfield Stables on Saturday morning and rode off on the stolen horse.

Witnesses described the thief as a blonde-haired man who had a beard and an earring in his right ear.

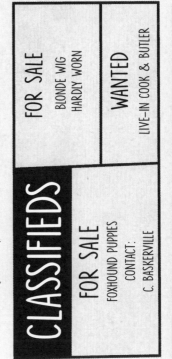
Above: Clanstar winning the Platinum Cup

The hunt continues to find the black car that thieves used after yesterday's bank heist.

But their plates didn't match, and no arrests were made.

Masked robbers fled the Sterling Bank in a vehicle, with the registration EU28, and disappeared into the Silver Mountain Tunnel. Police immediately closed the tunnel and found three black cars inside.

The mystery of the missing vehicle was further compounded by the discovery of several balls of scrunched up black tape nearby. Inspector Dodge however remains optimistic. "We have several hot leads, and we're certain to find the car before long."

None of the four men in custody matches the description, leading investigating officers to believe the thief could still be at large.

Public interest in the case remains high, not least because of the significant reward that Clanstar's owners have offered for information leading to the horse's recovery.

left: Arrested suspects so far:
Andy Tulip (top left),
Bernard Treacle (top right),
Cuthbert Chase (bottom left),
Danny Phantom (bottom right)

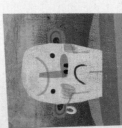

NU28 EU2l CL23

Above: Registration plates of the three vehicles found in the tunnel

CLASSIFIEDS

FOR SALE
FOXHOUND PUPPIES
CONTACT:
C. BASKERVILLE

FOR SALE
BLONDE WIG
HARDLY WORN

WANTED
LIVE-IN COOK & BUTLER

DRESS TO IMPRESS

Make and wear these costumes.

1 lay your hand over the edge of a piece of thick paper, like this.

Draw a big hand around yours.

2 Cut it out. Then, cut around it to make a second hand shape.

3 Wrap a strip of paper around your hand, and tape the ends to make a loop.

Stick the loop on one of the monster hands.

4 Tape the edges of the hands together, but leave the bottom open.

Repeat steps 1–4, to make another hand.

GIVE A MONSTER HANDSHAKE

Stick a paper claw on each finger.

Add paper spots, if you like.

BE A BUNCH OF GRAPES

Attach blue, red or purple balloons to an old sweater with safety pins behind the knots.

Did you know that grapes are a type of berry?

Yes, I heard it on the grapevine.

Complete the look with a headdress...

Cut leaf shapes out of green paper. Attach them to a headband with safety pins.

MAKE A FEROCIOUS LION MASK

1 First make a base...

Fold a piece of thick paper in half, then open it out. lay a pair of sunglasses over the fold, like this:

Draw around them.

2 Draw two ovals for eye holes inside the glasses shape. Pinch and snip into each oval to cut them out.

3 Cut the sides of the paper so the bottom is narrower than the top.

Then add a face...

1 Cut out and glue on paper shapes to make the lion's face. You could use newspaper or any scrap paper.

2 To make the mane, fold five strips of newspaper like this:

3 Then, tape them to the back of the mask, around the edges.

HOW TO WEAR

Cut a thick paper band that fits around your head. It should overlap a little.

Tape the ends to make a loop. Then, tape it to the back of the mask just above the eye holes.

ROOAaaRRR!

41

PLAY GAMES WITH PEBBLES

If you have some pebbles or stones, then you can play all these games.

Hopscotch

Draw the grid on the ground with chalk. Then, play this game on your own or in a group taking turns. If you step on a line, stumble or put the wrong foot down, you have to start again.

The grid

1 Throw a pebble onto square 1. Hop over square 1, and land on 2 on one foot...

2 Hop again and land with your left foot on square 3 and your right on 4...

3 Hop onto 5, 6 and 7, then hop onto 8. Jump around, then hop back to 2. Pick up the pebble...

4 Then hop onto 1 and hop off the end of the grid.

5 Next, throw the pebble onto square 2 before hopping along the grid. This time you have to hop over square 2. Hop back, stopping at squares 3 and 4 to pick up the pebble.

6 Keep playing until you have thrown the pebble onto all the squares. Hop up and down the grid each time. Remember to hop over the square that the pebble is on and pick it up on your way back.

On target

Any number of players can play this game, but first you need to make a target...

1 Stick two sheets of newspaper together with tape.

2 Draw a small circle in the middle before adding two bigger circles around it.

Write numbers on the target for scores.

You could draw the target in damp sand if you're on a sandy beach.

3 Then, try to throw pebbles inside the target's rings.

42

Nim

Nim is a game for two players.

1

Place 16 pebbles in four rows like this:

2

Take turns removing as many pebbles as you like – but only from one row at a time. The winner is the person who forces the loser to pick up the last pebble.

If you've got no pebbles, you can even play Nim with a pen and paper. Draw circles in rows and cross them out, to take them away.

How many in hand?

Hide up to five pebbles in your hand and make a fist. Then, challenge people to say how many you're holding. If they guess correctly, they score a point. If not, you score instead. Keep playing until someone has scored 5 points.

Try to trick your opponents...

Make a fist with an empty hand.

Squeeze your hand tightly or gently, to disguise how many pebbles you're holding.

Toss, pick up, catch

Play this game on your own using one hand only.

Keep your other hand behind your back.

The ancient Romans and Greeks played a game like this with small bones from the legs of sheep, called astragalus bones.

1
Place five pebbles on a table in front of you.

2
Toss a pebble in the air, then quickly pick up another pebble and catch the first pebble before it lands.

3
Put one pebble aside.

4
Repeat steps 2 and 3 until you've picked up all the pebbles.

5
Now try tossing a pebble and picking up two, three or four pebbles together before catching the first.

This game is also known as jacks or fives.

WATCH BIRDS

Make a bird feeder to attract birds to look at. You'll need a pinecone, string, peanut butter and some bird seed.

MAKE A BIRD FEEDER

1 Tie a piece of string around the top of a pinecone.

2 Spread peanut butter on the pinecone. Then, roll it in bird seed.

3 Hang the feeder from a branch.

You could use a cardboard tube instead of a pinecone, though it won't last as long.

Try to keep very still and quiet.

Birds may behave differently if they know you're watching them.

CAW CAW
(crow)

Start a bird log book and record everything you see and hear.

Describe each bird's markings and the way its beak looks.

Remember to write down the date and time, too.

HOW BIRDS BEHAVE

Thousands of starlings swoop and dive in time together. This is called a murmuration.

Gulls scare predators by flying at them noisily. This is called mobbing.

Gulls **squawk**, **squeal** and **laugh**.

EEEEK
Some owls **hoo hoo**, but barn owls like this one **shriek**.

Owls can't move their eyes, but they can turn their heads almost all the way around.

coo coo coo

Baby pigeons are known as squabs.

Adult pigeons coo to call each other back to the nest.

ooorhhh
A pigeon makes a sound like this when it's scared.

Gulls and other water birds have webbed feet for swimming.

QUACK WACK WAAACK

Ducks that live in noisy cities quack more loudly than ducks in the countryside.

Not all ducks **quack**. Some **whistle**, **coo**, **yodel** or **grunt**.

TCHILPPP
(sparrow)

ESCAPE FROM THE CASTLE

Follow the arrows and solve the puzzles to break free from the prison tower. Check the answers on the answer pages as you go.

Terence the Terrible

START HERE

Prison food

First, which path is safe to cross? These clues about the dragons will help you figure it out.

Paw and Claw would eat you up.
Fire is a vegetarian.
Claw guards the middle path.
Claw and Fire have wings.

Juliet the jester

Gardenia the gardener

Wrinkle the wizard is brewing a potion. Find the ingredients on these pages before continuing on your way.

INGREDIENTS

PINK FLOWER
CANNED TOMATOES
COBWEBS
BALL AND CHAIN
BLUE HAIR

Cindy's lost shoe

PEEKPU ELTSAC
SKIAPER TRAPMAR
DLROW GNIDRAZIW
DLO FO SEGCO
ZA SNOGARD

SKENNIGER ROF ERUTROT
GNITSIOT TA NIW OT WOH
EGASSAP NEPO OT KOOB HSUP
SLEWEJ NWORC ROF GNIRAC

A bookcase of odd-looking books blocks your way.

Decipher the titles to discover how to get past.

If you do the dishes, I'll let you pass. How long will it take you?

TIMES
2 MINUTES PER PLATE
1 MINUTE PER TANKARD
5 MINUTES PER SERVING PLATTER

Geoff the chef

Olf the ogre
If yesterday's tomorrow was Thursday, what day is the day after tomorrow's yesterday? Answer correctly and I won't eat you.
Lever
HAPPY BIRTHDAY PRINCE PERFECT!
I'll shout for the guards, unless you can find a way to slice my cake into 7 pieces, using only 3 straight lines. Draw a circle for the cake on a piece of paper and add lines as you try to find a solution.
Perfect's presents
Which way should you turn the lever to trap this monster – right or left?
Irritable ivy
Almost there... Only one hand wheel lowers the drawbridge. It's the odd one out. Which one is it? Clue: count the handles.
Sid the squid
YOU'VE ESCAPED!

DRAW A MENAGERIE

Follow the steps to draw a collection, or menagerie, of different wild animals.
You could fill them in with pens or crayons if you like.

Meerkat

1 Draw a hexagon like this.

2 Add a long body...

3 two arms...

4 two ears... a tail... legs...

A group of meerkats is called a mob.

5 two eye patches... two front paws... two back paws...

6 eyes, a nose and a mouth. Add squiggles for fur.

Zebra

1 Draw a long rectangle...

2 a neck... a head...

3 two ears... a nose...

4 a mane... four legs...

5 lots of stripes... a tail... two eyes... and nostrils too.

48

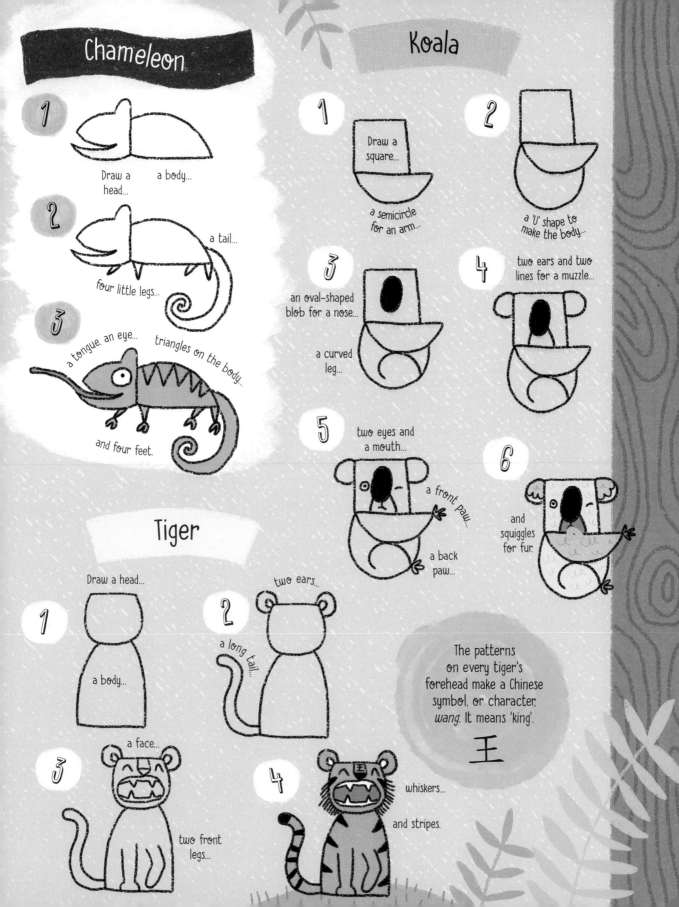

Chameleon

1 Draw a head... a body...

2 four little legs... a tail...

3 a tongue, an eye... triangles on the body. and four feet.

Koala

1 Draw a square... a semicircle for an arm...

2 a 'U' shape to make the body...

3 an oval-shaped blob for a nose... a curved leg...

4 two ears and two lines for a muzzle...

5 two eyes and a mouth... a front paw... a back paw...

6 and squiggles for fur.

Tiger

1 Draw a head... a body...

2 two ears... a long tail...

3 a face... two front legs...

4 whiskers... and stripes.

The patterns on every tiger's forehead make a Chinese symbol, or character, *wang*. It means 'king'.

王

MAKE ICE CUBE TREATS

You need an ice cube tray to make these recipes.
They will take around two hours to freeze in a freezer.

MANGO DREAMS

Blend two handfuls of canned or ripe mango in a blender. Spoon the mixture into your tray and freeze.

FROZEN CHEESECAKE

Break two ginger snaps or chocolate cookies into crumbs. Add a teaspoon of crumbs into each hole in the tray. Next, fill the holes with any yogurt you like before freezing.

STRAWBERRY SUNSET

Mash ten ripe strawberries with a fork in a bowl. Add five tablespoons of plain yogurt and one teaspoon of honey. Stir together, then freeze in a tray.

Tip: If you don't have a blender, you can crush the mango with the bottom of a mug on a chopping board.

Try concocting your own recipes, and thinking up names for them.

NOW TRY MAKING STRIPED CUBES...

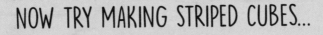

Pour a little juice, smoothie or yogurt into the holes in an ice cube tray. Then freeze for an hour.

Next, add a second, different layer and freeze for another hour.

Keep adding and freezing layers until the holes are full.

BUILD A SNOWMAN
(even in summer)

FIRST MAKE 'SNOW'

Pour six tablespoons of baking powder into a mixing bowl.

Slowly stir in four squirts of shaving foam until you have an even mixture.

Roll it into two or more snowballs.

You could put your snowballs in the fridge for an hour to make them cold, if you like.

NOW MAKE A MINI SNOWMAN

Use two snowballs for a head and a body...

two peppercorns for eyes

a sliver of carrot for a nose

tiny twigs for arms

ribbon for a scarf

jassa

borga

guoldu

SNOWY WORDS

The Sami people, who live in the most northern parts of Europe, have more than 180 words to describe snow and ice.

How many words that start with 'snow' can you make using the letters on the right? You can reuse letters for each new word.

SNOW...

H	A	S
K		T
	R	
I	F	M	L
E		B
	O	P
D	N	L

Which one of these snowy facts is not true?

Every single snowflake is unique.

Snow isn't white – it's transparent. It looks white because of the way light bounces off it.

Snow houses can be up to 60°C (140°F) warmer than the temperature outside, when people are inside them.

WRITE ABOUT A QUEST

A quest is a long search for something that's difficult to find.
Take a look at some of the quest stories below,
then try writing one of your own.

The Quest for the Holy Grail

One of the oldest, most famous, quest stories is the
Quest for the Holy Grail – a magical cup that's said
to grant eternal youth to whoever drinks from it.

The story – which was retold many times
during the Middle Ages – follows the adventures
of the legendary British ruler, King Arthur, and
his Knights of the Round Table.

Which book?

Have you read any of the following
quest stories? Match each book cover
to the short description of its plot.

1. A girl from Kansas and her dog
are swept away by a tornado
and taken to a magical land.
There's only one way home.

2. A curious young girl tumbles down
a rabbit hole after following a
white rabbit. She finds herself in
a bizarre fantasy world.

3. A small, hairy-footed character
inherits a magical object with
dark powers. He must do all he
can to destroy it.

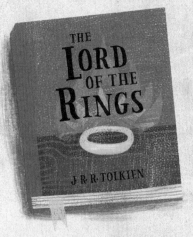

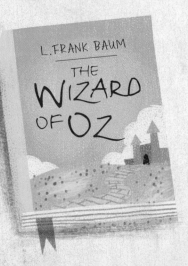

Dylan's quest

Write a story about a quest using the story map below.
Choose any route – long or short – and use the quest
words at the bottom of the page to help you.

START

When Dylan falls down a well, he finds himself trapped in a magical land. To get back home, he must find a magic ring.

Can this kindly old wizard help Dylan find the ring?

Watch out – a hairy monster! Does Dylan turn back or carry on?

A terrible storm blows in – where does Dylan take shelter?

BREAKNECK BRIDGE

How does Dylan get across Breakneck Bridge?

MURKY MOUNTAIN RANGE

Dylan spots a ladder as he walks along the mountain trail – is it a shortcut?

GOOEY GUNGE SWAMP

hi

A smelly, bubbling swamp is blocking Dylan's way. Can he swim through it?

Oh hello! Is this a friendly bear? Or is it hungry for some lunch?

Dylan finds the magic ring! What happens when he puts it on?

Quest words

Pursue BRAVE Threat DANGER FAIL COWARDLY

TERRIFYING HERO Task Goal Overcome Battle Seek

SUCCEED Perilous Distracted Heroine Defeat Labyrinth

53

MAKE A TELEPHONE

You can make a simple telephone with two paper cups and some string.

1 Make a small hole in the bottom of each cup with the point of a pencil.

2 Cut a very long piece of string. Thread one end through the hole in one of the cups. Tie a big knot inside.

3 Repeat with the other end of the string and the other cup. Your phone is now ready to use.

There's a spider on your head!!!

Ask someone to take a cup into another room, and speak into it.

Keep the string stretched very tight and don't let it touch anything.

Hold the other cup to your ear, to hear what the person is saying.

How does it work?

Talking vibrates the air in the cup. These vibrations travel along the string and can be heard as sounds at the other end.

TELEPHONE TIMELINE

The telephone was invented in 1876. It converted sounds into electrical signals and sent them down a wire.

Both Elisha Gray and Alexander Graham Bell separately developed the first telephones. But Bell's invention was recognized first.

From 1878, telephone exchanges linked together all the telephones in one area. Operators plugged in wires to connect different phones.

SAY HELLO...

Find out how to say "hello" and "goodbye" in lots of different languages.

DZYN DZYN

Poland

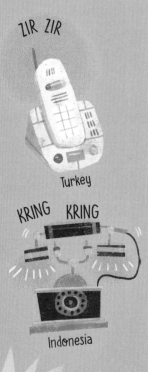

ZIR ZIR

Turkey

DRIN DRIN

Italy

KRING KRING

Indonesia

LANGUAGE	HELLO	GOODBYE
Croatian	Bok	Zbogom
Danish	Hej	Farvel
Dutch	Hallo	Doei
Estonian	Tere	Head aega
French	Bonjour	Au revoir
Hawaiian	Aloha	A hui hou
Irish	Dia dhuit	Slán
Italian	Ciao	Arrivederci
Lithuanian	Labas	Viso gero
Maori	Kia ora	Hei kona rā
Norwegian	Hei	Ha det bra
Romanian	Salut	la revedere
Slovak	Dobry den	Dovidenia
Swahili	Habari	Kwaheri

These are some of the words used around the world to describe the 'ring ring' sound made by telephones.

RIN RIN

Japan

DRING DRING

France

The year 1919 saw the first dial telephones. Each phone had a separate earpiece and mouthpiece to hold, so writing down messages was tricky.

In 1963, the first touch-tone telephones went on sale. Pushing buttons was faster and more accurate than turning a dial.

In 1984, handheld portable phones went on sale. Each phone was about the size of a brick. Its battery took ten hours to charge and lasted for just 30 minutes.

Egyptian kings' names were usually written in oval frames called *cartouches*, so I think this could be Ptolemy's name.

3 Champollion read the name of an Egyptian king called Ptolemy in the Ancient Greek. He guessed that the hieroglyphs contained the *same* message, so he looked for the symbols that might stand for 'Ptolemy'...

He compared it with another cartouche that was thought to contain the name of an Egyptian queen, Cleopatra.

5 Champollion studied other royal names, and decoded every hieroglyph. Here are the hieroglyphs that make similar sounds to the letters in the alphabet that we use.

A B C or C D E F G H

I J K or K L M or M N O

P Q R S T U V W

X Y Z

NOW...
Write your own name in hieroglyphs and draw a cartouche shape around it.

Aha!

Untranslatable?
Some ancient languages are still a mystery...

Byblic
(found in Lebanon)

Hattic
(from Turkey)

Iberic
(from Spain and Portugal)

READ THE CLOUDS

Use this cloud spotting guide below and look at the sky to tell whether it's going to rain or not.

Cirrus

High clouds

Probably no rain today!

Cirrocumulus

Cirrostratus

Mid-level clouds

It might rain in the next six to twelve hours.

Altocumulus

The Sun is visible through mid-level clouds.

Altostratus

The lower clouds are, the sooner the weather will change.

Low clouds

Rain is here – or on its way.

Cumulus

Cumulonimbus

Stratus

Cumulus clouds grow taller into cumulonimbus clouds when it's stormy.

Nimbostratus

Low clouds block out the Sun.

Cloud shapes

Sometimes clouds have strange shapes that remind you of other things. What shapes can you see in these photographs?

Thornham, August 17

You could keep your own log of the different clouds you see. Record where and when you spotted each one.

Sousse, July 5

"I spy with my little eye, a cloud shape beginning with 'h'..."

– If you're with friends when you spot a cloud that looks like something, you could challenge them to guess what.

Gdansk, September 15

Aosta, September 23

Odd clouds

Most cloud names come from five words in latin. You can tell what their names mean if you remember these five words.

cirrus – curl
stratus – layer
alto – high
cumulus – heap
nimbus – cloud

So, for example, cirrocumulus means 'a heap of curls'.

Lenticular clouds are sometimes mistaken for UFOs.

Nacreous clouds have a pearly sheen.

Mammatus clouds look lumpy and sometimes appear before storms.

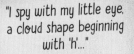

FIND WORDS

Write a list of all the words you find in this grid. Join as many letters together as you can – so long as they are next to each other.

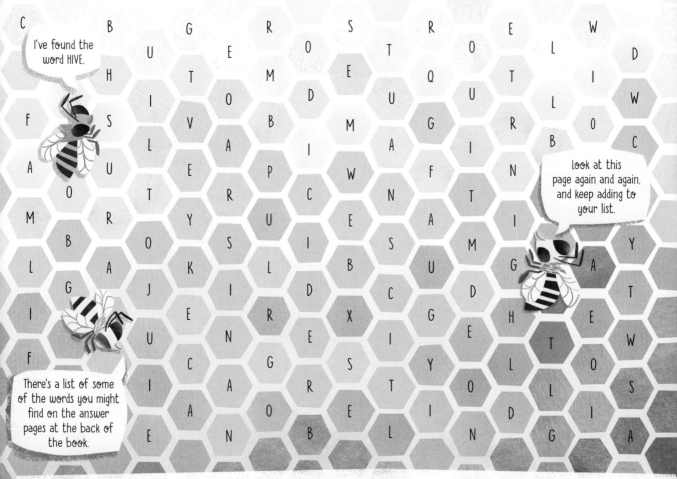

I've found the word HIVE.

Look at this page again and again, and keep adding to your list.

There's a list of some of the words you might find on the answer pages at the back of the book.

NOW INVENT YOUR OWN WORDS...

New words are known as neologisms. Read these examples to help you make up your own.

Write a mini dictionary of all your words. Remember to include a definition for each one.

punge

adjective – very smelly, pungent

• Shorten a word to make a new one.

BIf

adjective – a phone or any electronic device when its Battery Is Flat

This word is an acronym – each letter stands for a different word.

whispurr

verb – to speak quietly like a cat

blurple

noun – a shade that's neither blue nor purple

This type of neologism – when parts of words are combined together – is known as a portmanteau.

TEST YOUR MEMORY [PART 1]

Look at these pictures for a few minutes, and try to remember as much as you can about these superheroes.

TIP: Using different parts of your brain helps you to remember things. For example...

- Read the names aloud. Listen to how they sound.
- Imagine why they might have their names.

Stretchy

Blaze

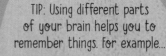

Lionel

Scarlet

Brawn

Stormy

Swoop

Invisa

When you're ready, turn the page.

TEST YOUR MEMORY (PART 2)

How many of these superheroes' names can you remember?

Only look at this page when you've read the page before.

WHOOSH!

BOOF!

BOOM!

BANG!

Which hero is missing?

WHIZZ!

Now try... list learning

Look at this shopping list for 30 seconds, then close the book. Try to write the items down in the same order.

Shopping list

TIP: To help you remember, imagine eating all the items on this list.

- Banana
- Carrots
- Bread
- Cherry cake
- Broccoli
- Red Onion
- Rice
- Peas

Play 'Pairs'

This memory game is for any number of players.

1 Shuffle a deck of 52 playing cards and lay them out face down in four rows of 13 cards.

2 The first player turns over two cards. If they are the same shade and value, such as two red queens, the player keeps the cards and has another turn. If the cards don't match, the cards are turned face down in the same place.

3 The game continues with players taking turns to find pairs until all the cards have been picked up. The winner is the player with the most pairs.

REMEMBER A ROUTINE

Make up a dance sequence in a group, then see who can bust the most moves in the right order.

1 The first person makes up a dance move.

You could raise your arms and move them in a circle.

2 The next person copies the first dance move and adds a new one.

What about adding a jump?

3 Everyone takes turns performing the dance moves and adding another each time.

You're OUT if you forget a dance move in the sequence. The last person still dancing wins the game.

Maybe clap your hands and lift your leg.

DANCE MOVE IDEAS

Disco fever

Point at your hip, and then up in the air.

Jazz twist

Touch your elbow and twirl your other hand.

Under the sea

Pinch your nose and wave your fingers across your face.

Funky chicken

Flap your arms up and down.

Mashed potato

Bang your fists together twice, then swap hands and repeat.

GROW GREENS FROM SCRAPS

Did you know that some of the ends and tops left over when you prepare vegetables and salads can grow again?

lettuce

1 Stand the end of a lettuce upright in a small bowl of shallow water.

2 Leave the bowl on a sunny windowsill. Change the water every day or two, as the lettuce grows new leaves.

3 After a week or so, the leaves should be big enough to cut and eat.

Salad onions

Stand spring onions (also known as green onions) with their roots in a jar of water. Cut off the leaves as you need them. They'll grow back after a few days.

You could reuse an old plastic container instead of a jar.

Cut up any greens you've grown and add them to salads.

Carrot tops

If you stand the top of a carrot in some water, it will grow green leaves.

TAKE CUTTINGS

You can turn one basil or mint plant into *several* plants.
For each new plant you want to grow...

1
Cut a leafy stem from the plant. Pull off a few leaves, so the bottom of the stem is bare.

2
Stand the stem in a jar or glass of water. Leave it on a sunny windowsill and wait for roots to grow.

3
When the roots are about 2cm (1in) long, fill a small pot with compost. Make a hole with your finger and plant the stem.

Make your own pesto

Basil is the main ingredient of pesto – a tasty sauce that can be stirred through pasta. It's equally delicious spread on toasted bread.

Ingredients

3 handfuls of basil leaves

1 small clove of garlic, peeled

a handful of pinenuts

a glug of olive oil

a handful of grated, hard Italian cheese

a pinch of salt

Serves 4

Method

Either...
Blend all the ingredients in a blender until you have a smooth paste.

Or...
Use the base of a mug to smush the basil, garlic, pinenuts and salt together on a chopping board...

....before mixing with the oil and cheese in a bowl.

Pesto takes its name from an Italian word *pestare* that means 'to crush'.

No two handfuls are the same...

When you make recipes like pesto you don't have to measure the amount of each ingredient you use too precisely.

65

STARGAZE

There are thousands of stars you can see* at night, even without a telescope.

Constellations

Early astronomers grouped stars into pictures called constellations. They named them after animals, objects and heroes from myths.

Clear, cloudless nights are best for stargazing.

Crux, also known as the Southern Cross, always points south.

Orion is named after a hunter from a Greek myth. He looks as if he's carrying a sword and a shield.

Shooting stars are actually space rocks that burn up as they travel through the Earth's atmosphere. They're also known as meteors.

Sometimes planets are visible too. Mars has a reddish glow.

You can often see the planet Venus early in the morning near the horizon.

You can tell planets apart from stars because planets don't twinkle, but stars do.

Jupiter, the largest planet in the Solar System, looks very big and bright.

*What you *see* depends on the time of year and where you are in the world.

Now try Moongazing

The Moon looks as if it changes shape because different parts of it are lit up by the Sun as it moves around the Earth.

The Moon *seems* to appear and then disappear every 29.5 days.

day 1   day 7   day 15   day 23   day 29

There are dark patches on the Moon's surface known as **maria**. They were made when volcanoes on the Moon erupted long, long ago.

Moongazers around the world imagine different pictures in these patches. What do you see when you look at the full Moon?

A rabbit mashing rice (China and Japan)

A man carrying a bundle of wood (parts of Europe)

Handprints (India)

A frog or a toad (parts of Africa and North America)

The Plough / Big Dipper

If you're facing north outside at night, you can sometimes see the North Star shining above the North Pole.

The Pleiades, or Seven Sisters, have a bluish glow. They make up the largest group of stars you can see with your own eyes.

RACE PENGUINS

To play this game, each player needs a small coin to use as a penguin counter. If you don't have a dice, you can find out how to make one on page 28.

START!

Roll the dice to decide who starts. The person with the highest score goes first.

A tasty meal of fish gives you an energy boost. Move forward 1 space.

Killer whales jiggle this ice float. Move back 1 space.

Wandering albatrosses have the longest wingspan of any bird – over 3m (10ft).

An albatross shows you a shortcut. Roll again!

In winter, the sea around Antarctica freezes, doubling the size of the continent.

Move back 2 spaces to hide from a hungry seal.

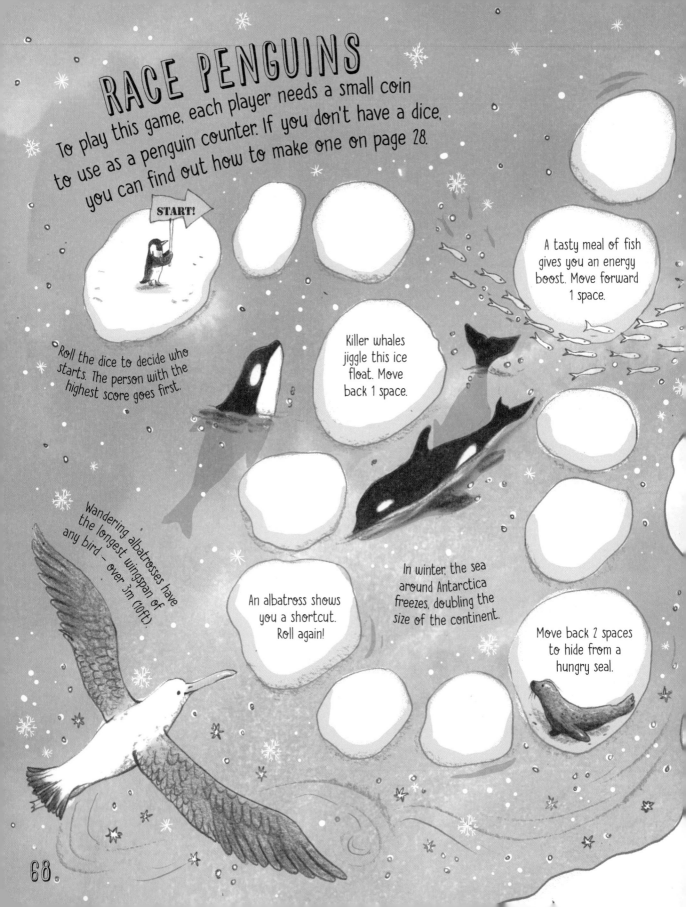

You fall off this ice float. Throw a 3 to get back on.

You get caught in a blizzard and walk the wrong way. Go back 1 space.

You help a lost chick find its parents. They push you on 1 space.

Emperor penguins recognize their chicks by the sound of their calls.

Emperor penguins live in huge colonies of up to 40,000 penguins.

You stop to talk to a friend. Miss a turn.

SLIPPERY

Slip back 3 spaces.

FINISH!

Hitch a ride on a snow mobile and jump forward 3 spaces.

Now...

You could make your own board game with a different theme. Draw a path of 25 spaces or more, then write on different instructions using the ideas above.

MAKE GIANT BUBBLES

How big a bubble can you blow with this wand and bubble mixture?

For the bubble wand, you will need...

① Cut the top ends of two straws, so they're slanted.

② Insert the slanted end of each straw into another straw, to make two longer straws.

Some string

4 plastic straws

Scissors

③ Cut a piece of string, about 25cm (10in) long, and another piece twice as long.

For the bubble mixture...

Slowly mix together in a bucket:

6 cups of cool water

1/4 cup of dishwashing liquid

④ Tie the short string between the tops of both straws. Then tie the long string to either end of the short string, to make a loop.

short string

long string

Make bubbles...

① Dip your wand into the mixture and move it around.

② Wave your wand through the air gently to make bubbles appear.

It's best to make bubbles outside.

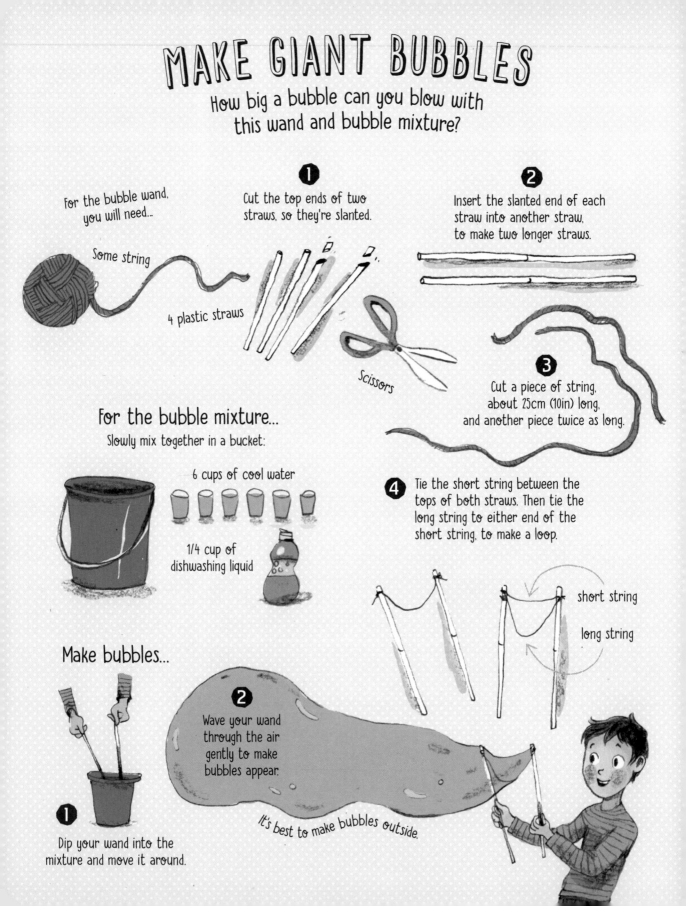

Now try... blowing bubbles from a bottle

Carefully cut the bottom end off a plastic bottle.

Dip the cut end in a tray of bubble mixture.

Blow through the neck of the bottle to make a bubble.

Did you know that you can also make bubbles within bubbles?

Bubble mixture

How many bubbles within bubbles can you blow?

1 Dip a straw into some bubble mixture. A little of the mixture will go up the straw.

2 Blow very gently through the straw onto a plate, until you've made a big bubble.

3 Take out the straw. Then, poke it back through, and blow bubbles inside the big bubble.

'Bubbleology'*

The biggest floating soap bubble ever recorded was 182 times bigger than a party balloon.

Some fish build nests of bubbles, made from their spit, to protect their eggs.

In some places at low temperatures, you can spot frozen bubbles of methane gas underwater.

Bubbles in lava make volcanoes explode very violently.

*The study of bubbles

UNLOCK SECRETS OF THE MIND

People who study how people think and behave are called psychologists. You can carry out your own psychological investigation with this inkblot test.

Swiss psychologist Hermann Rorschach (1884-1922) was the first person to use inkblots to investigate people's minds.

He thought people revealed their secret thoughts when he asked them to say what they saw in the shapes.

Make an inkblot

You'll need:
• black paint or ink
• thick paper
• a paintbrush

1

Fold a piece of paper in half, and then unfold it.

2

Use a paintbrush to drip thick lines and blobs of paint or ink into the middle of the paper.

3

Fold the paper in half again and press down.

4

Unfold the paper and leave it to dry.

The test

Look at your inkblot for no longer than 10 seconds.

Write down what you see in the shapes – an object perhaps, or an animal.

Give the first answer that comes into your head.

Ask other people to look at the inkblot and record what they see, too.

Now... examine the answers

Here are some possible answers for the inkblot on the left and ideas for different meanings behind them.

"Someone reading a book"

You may find lots of people give the same answers. Great minds think alike.

"Someone looking in terror at the homework they forgot to do"

Detailed answers might indicate creativity. But are they talking about the inkblot – or themselves?

"It's an inkblot."

This is an obvious answer, but not very imaginative. People who give answers like this may be trying to hide their real thoughts from you.

"It's a man-eating book!"

People who see terrifying monsters in every inkblot sound like worriers. Could there be something on their minds?

"(silence)"

Difficult to say... Was the person you asked awake?

If you don't have paint or ink, you could close your eyes and doodle squiggles and blobs instead. Then, you can use the picture you made for the test.

MAKE A FLIPBOOK MOVIE

Here's how to make your own animation. You'll need a piece of plain paper, some pencils, scissors and a clip.

Fold a rectangular piece of paper in half this way once.

Then fold it in half this way...

...three times.

Cut along the fold lines to make 16 identical strips of paper.

Then, choose either the 'jumping man' or 'flying bird' animation below. Copy or trace the pictures in each square frame onto the right-hand half of the 16 strips (see below).

THE JUMPING MAN

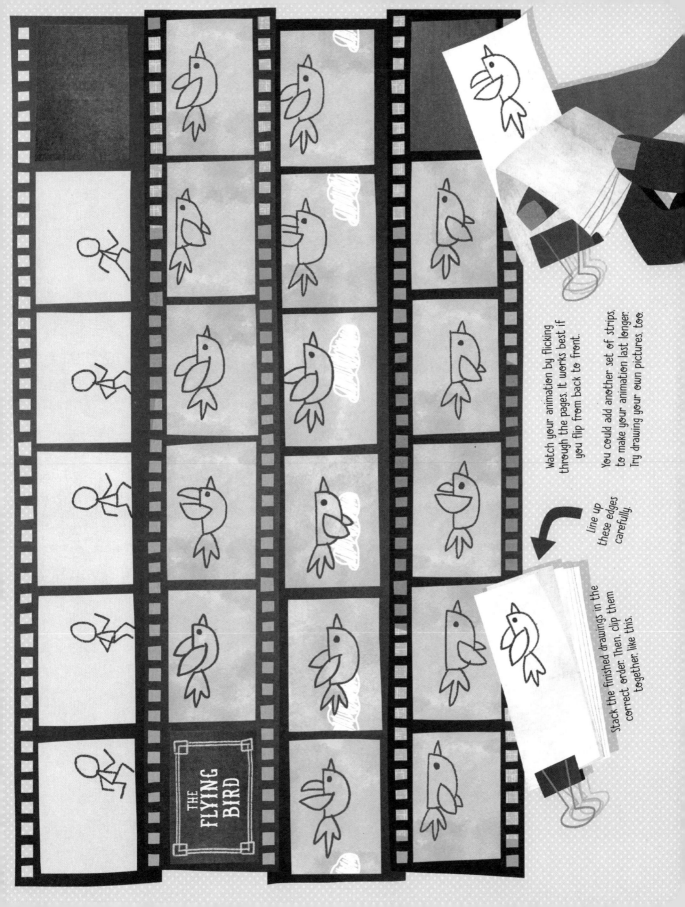

THE FLYING BIRD

Watch your animation by flicking through the pages. It works best if you flip from back to front.

You could add another set of strips, to make your animation last longer. Try drawing your own pictures, too.

line up these edges carefully.

Stack the finished drawings in the correct order. Then, clip them together, like this.

QUESTION EVERYTHING

Quiz yourself or your friends with these questions.

1 Which animal has the most powerful bite?
   a) Crocodile
   b) Grizzly bear
   c) Great white shark

2 What is a coccyx (say 'kok-siks')?
   a) A small flying dinosaur
   b) The 'tailbone' at the bottom of the human spine
   c) An ancient Greek game

3 Which of the following creatures are *not* used by doctors today?
   a) Ants
   b) leeches
   c) Maggots

4 When it was completed in 1889, the Eiffel Tower was the tallest structure in the world. True or false?

5 How many sides does a nonagon have?
   a) None
   b) Nine
   c) Ninety

6 Which Roman emperor is said to have played his fiddle while Rome burned?
   a) Nero   b) Caligula   c) Tiberius

7 A rattlesnake cannot hear its own rattle. True or false?

8 Humans have more bones when they are babies than when they are grown ups. True or false?

9 If you sneeze in Germany, what would someone say?
   a) Schnitzel!   b) À tes souhaits!   c) Gesundheit!

10 Which of the Earth's poles has land beneath the ice?
   a) North Pole   b) South Pole   c) Both!

11 Where would you find the Shaolin Monastery, where some of the world's best martial arts experts were trained?
   a) Thailand
   b) China
   c) Japan

12 How should you deal with a charging rhino?
   a) Keep quiet and throw a rock to one side
   b) Shout and scream as loudly as you can
   c) Punch it on the nose

13 Where is your blood made?
   a) In your heart
   b) In your lungs
   c) In your bones

14 How many bacteria live in your body?
   a) A few, but only when you're ill
   b) A thousand
   c) One hundred trillion

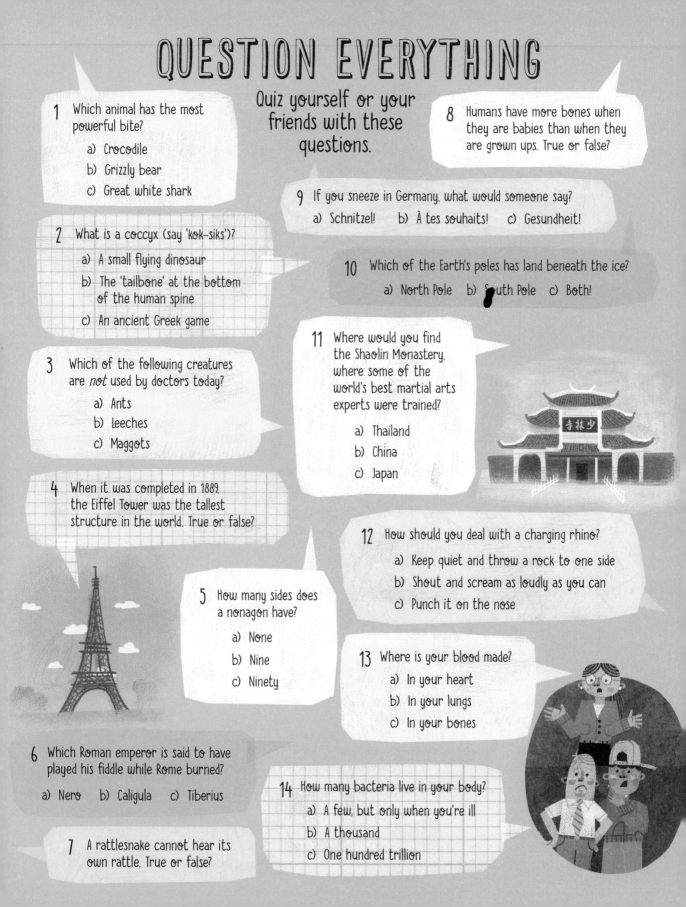

15 What is the name of the huge river that begins in Peru and flows through dense rainforest without being crossed by a single bridge?

    a) The Amazon   b) The Nile   c) The Seine

24 What is a group of crows called?

    a) A funeral

    b) A murder

    c) A swarm

16 What is the biggest living thing on planet Earth?

    a) A giant redwood tree

    b) A honey fungus

    c) A blue whale

25 Which of these is not a real element?

    a) Argon   b) Chlorine   c) Kryptonite

17 How many teeth did the dinosaur Triceratops have?

    a) 80   b) 800   c) 8,000

26 In the past, how did sailors on long voyages avoid getting a deadly disease called scurvy?

    a) Slept for an extra hour a night

    b) Ate lemons

    c) Rubbed honey into their skin

18 What type of animal is a bat?

    a) Bird   b) Mammal   c) Reptile

27 What is a baby kangaroo called?

    a) A joey   b) A sheila   c) A billy

19 Identical twins have the same fingerprints. True or false?

28 Who wrote *Wuthering Heights*?

    a) Charlotte Brontë

    b) Emily Brontë

    c) Catherine Heathcliff

20 What is the largest country in the world?

    a) Australia   b) China   c) Russia

21 What is Eyjafjallajökull?

    a) A made-up word

    b) An album released by the singer Björk in 2014

    c) An Icelandic volcano

29 Which has the longest tail?

    a) Sloth

    b) Indian elephant

    c) Giraffe

22 Stephen Hawking invented the World Wide Web. True or false?

30 You're on a beach in Italy and someone says to you "I tuoi piedi puzzano di formaggio!" What does it mean?

    a) The water is very pleasant!

    b) Your feet smell like cheese!

    c) I've got sand in my trunks!

23 Which is further from Earth, Neptune or Venus?

ROMANO MORE VIVE*

* This means 'live like a Roman' in Latin – the language most ancient Romans spoke.

latine loquere*

Try learning some Latin, then you'll be able to read the story at the bottom of this page.

salve (sal–vay)	hello	puella	girl
vale (val–ay)	goodbye	puer	boy
gratias ago	thank you	mater	mother
non scio	I don't know	pater	father
ut vales?	how are you?	frater	brother
bene valeo	I'm well	soror	sister
optime	very well	ubi est...?	where is...?
pessime	terrible	in foro	at the market
quod nomen tibi est?	what's your name?	in schola	at school
mihi nomen est...	my name is...	te amo	I love you

*Speak latin

Nunc hanc fabulam lege*

salve, mater. ubi est Hector?

non scio.

salve, pater. ubi est Hector?

non scio.

salve, soror. ubi est Hector?

non scio.

salve, frater. ubi est Hector?

non scio.

o Hector, te amo!

*Now read this story

Usque ad decem numera*

The Romans wrote letters for numbers. You'll find the Latin words for one to ten below too.

1	I	unus
2	II	duo
3	III	tres
4	IV	quatuor
5	V	quinque
6	VI	sex
7	VII	septem
8	VIII	octo
9	IX	novem
10	X	decem

*Count to ten

Togam gere*

Use a bed sheet for a toga.

1. Wear a belt over a T-shirt. Drape the toga over your left shoulder.

2. Wrap the right side across your body...

3. ...and over your shoulder.

4. Then, tuck the end into your belt.

*Wear a toga

Alea lude*

This game for two players is based on Rock, Paper, Scissors.

Players count to three before saying the name of a type of gladiator and making a shape with their right hand for the weapon that gladiator used.

pugil (boxing glove)

....

retiarius (net)

....

secutor (sword)

Pugil beats secutor.
Retiarius beats pugil.
Secutor beats retiarius.

*Play a game

Inventores magni*

Did you know the Romans invented...?

concrete

arches

underfloor heating

flushing toilets

tower blocks

surgical tools

*Great inventors

CUT A SILHOUETTE

A silhouette is a solid-shape portrait of a person seen from the side. You'll need a photo that shows the shapes of a person's nose, chin and other features clearly.

1 Cut very carefully around the edges of the person's head and upper body. This is your template.

Silhouettes first became popular as cheap alternatives to painted portraits over 200 years ago. They're named after a penny-pinching French politician, Étienne de Silhouette.

2 Stick the template on a piece of black paper with sticky tape over all its edges. Then, cut carefully around the edge of the template.

3 The template will come away from the black paper, leaving a solid shape – a silhouette. Stick it on a piece of plain or patterned paper.

Now try this...

You could stick on shapes for extra details such as windows.

You can make 'silhouettes' of objects, animals and scenes too. Cut out any pictures you like. Then stick them on paper and cut them out again.

Silhouette spotting

Scan the crowd of silhouettes below. Which can you spot more of: beards, ponytails or glasses?

Name words

Words (like silhouette) that originally come from people's names are known as eponyms. Here are some more...

diesel ♫

braille

fuchsia

atlas

saxophone

guillotine

leotard

mausoleum

begonia

look them up in a big dictionary to find out about the people they're named after...

SET UP A BOWLING ALLEY

find some empty plastic bottles and
try to knock them down with a ball.

1. READY

Collect up to ten plastic bottles and a small ball. The bottles don't have to be the same size or look the same.

You score a point for every bottle you knock down.

The player with the highest number of points at the end of the game wins.

2. SET

Mark out a long lane on a smooth floor with strips of masking tape.

Before each player's turn, set up the empty bottles in a pyramid shape, leave little gaps between them.

STRIKE

If you knock down all the bottles on your first roll of the ball, it is called a strike.

+5 bonus points!

3. GO!

Players take turns trying to knock down as many bottles as they can. They get two rolls of the ball each turn. The ball has to stay inside the lane.

Or try this...

If you only have one bottle, you could set it up at the end of a lane and try to knock it down.

PLAY RING TOSS

Here's another game to play with the bottles you collected for the bowling alley.

First you need to make two rings for each player.

To make a ring...

1

Draw around a plate on a piece of thick paper.

2

Cut out the circle. Then, fold it in half.

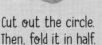

3

Cut out a semi-circle shape, about the width of two fingers in from the edge.

4

Unfold to reveal a ring.

RING CHALLENGE

With your finger, can you draw a route through all the rings below, using only four straight lines and without taking your finger off the page?

Start

Tip: think outside the box.

Fill four plastic bottles with water. This makes them heavy, so that they don't fall over.

Players try to throw their rings over the bottles.

The player with the most successful throws wins!

BECOME A WILD ARTIST

Make wild works of art using leaves, sticks,
pebbles, sand or mud next time you're outside.

PEBBLE PATTERNS

Arrange pebbles in
meandering lines.

LEAF CIRCLES

Use fallen leaves
to make circular,
starburst patterns.

! Don't pick leaves
while they're still
on a tree.

FOOTPRINT FLOWERS

Turn around on the spot moving
one foot at a time, to make
prints in mud or sand.

PENGUIN PRINTS

Walk with your feet pointing
at angles, like a penguin.

BARK RUBBING

Place a piece of paper against a tree trunk
and rub over it with a wax crayon.

STICK LINES

You could create
patterns with twigs you
find on the ground.

Now use all the different
techniques together to make
a BIG work of outdoor art.

BE A DINOSAUR DETECTIVE

Can you identify these dinosaurs from the clues below?

A plant-eater
length: 11m (36ft)

B plant-eater
length: 10m (33ft)

C plant-eater
length: 5.5m (18ft)

D meat-eater
length: 10m (33ft)

E meat-eater
length: 12m
(40ft)

Tyrannosaurus has the shortest arms.

Allosaurus is the same length as **Parasaurolophus**.

Styracosaurus has the most horns and is half the length of **Triceratops**.

Parasaurolophus stands on two legs and eats plants.

EVERYONE MAKES MISTAKES...

In 1868, American scientist Edward Drinker Cope put together the first set of Elasmosaurus bones ever found. But he accidentally attached its head to its tail.

I look ridiculous!

Elasmosaurus is a type of plesiosaur that lived in the sea about 80 million years ago.

Drinker Cope thought that Elasmosaurus had a short neck and a long tail.

In fact, it had a long neck and a short tail.

85

WRITE A ZINE

Make, write and publish your own mini magazine, or 'zine'.

1

Fold a piece of paper in half, short edge to short edge.

2

Fold it in half again long edge to long edge, and then again short edge to short edge.

3

Undo step 2. The paper should be creased like this.

4

Carefully cut along this crease.

STOP HERE

FILL THE PAGES

Your zine could be about anything - pets, robots, cars, superheroes...

Once you've chosen a topic, fill the pages with doodles, stories, jokes...

Monster of the Month

FRANKENFUZZ

BOO!

ROAR

SQUEAK

GNASH

THE MONSTER TIMES

INSIDE:
furry quiz, beastly rhymes and monster portraits

Give your zine a title.

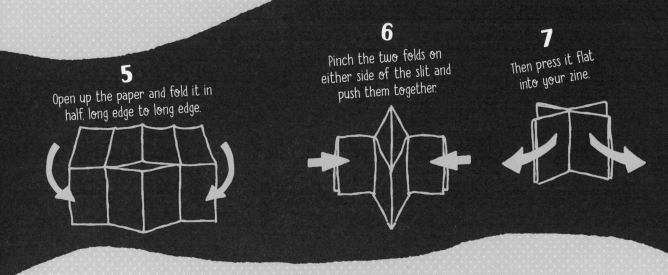

5

Open up the paper and fold it in half, long edge to long edge.

6

Pinch the two folds on either side of the slit and push them together.

7

Then press it flat into your zine.

MAKE A COMIC FOR YOUR ZINE

You don't need amazing drawing skills. Just start with stick figures.

Most comics take place inside boxes called panels. You don't have to show all of the action – just the most important or exciting parts.

PUBLISH IT!

Lend your zine to anyone who wants to read it. If you have access to a scanner and a printer, you can make copies to fold and hand out.

Zines are cheap and easy to distribute, so people use them to share ideas and campaign for things.

What will your zine be about?

Joke of the Week

OMG

SAVE OUR LIBRARY

BAFFLE YOUR EYES
Give these mind-bending optical illusions a try.

WHIRLING CIRCLES

Move your eyes around, and the circles will start to spin.

HOW MANY PRONGS?

This impossible shape looks like it has both two *and* three prongs at the same time.

WONKY SQUARES?

The diagonal lines make the squares look as if they're slanting in different directions, but they are completely regular.

SLANTING LINES

The lines seem to tilt but they are horizontal.

DANCING DOTS

Black dots appear to dance around, but all the dots are actually white.

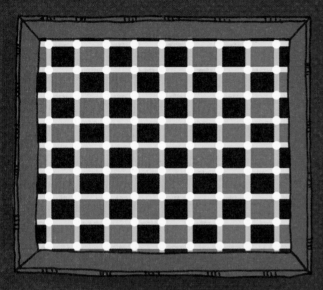

TILTING HEXAGONS

The green lines in both shapes line up perfectly. See for yourself by checking them with a ruler.

SAME SHADES?

The patches on both giraffes are exactly the same shade. Changing the background tricks the brain into thinking they're different.

If you don't believe it cup your hands around each giraffe and look closely.

HOW DO THEY WORK?

Optical illusions work by tricking your brain into seeing something that isn't there.

Faced with confusing information, your brain jumps to conclusions and imagines things.

FOLD A BOAT

Follow these steps to make an origami
model of a sampan – a type of flat-bottomed Chinese boat.
You'll need a square piece of paper for each sampan.

How to make a square

1. Fold one corner of a rectangular piece of paper to the opposite edge.

2. Use a ruler to draw a line at the bottom edge of the triangle, then cut along the line.

3. Unfold the triangle to reveal the square.

TO MAKE A SAMPAN

1

Fold the paper in half from bottom to top and unfold it.

2

Fold up the bottom edge and fold down the top edge to meet the middle crease.

3

Fold in each of the four corners to the middle.

4

Now fold the bottom-left edge into the middle.

In 2015, engineers in London made a large paper boat that was strong enough to carry a person across a lake.

'Origami' comes from the Japanese words for 'fold' (ori) and 'paper' (kami).

90

5

Fold in the other
three edges, too.

6

Fold the top and bottom
points into the middle.

7

Lift up all of the flaps on
either side of the middle
line to open up the model.

8

Then turn the whole thing
inside out. Flatten the base
of the sampan.

9

Flip over for the
finished sampan.

Now try this...

Before floating your boat on water, first make
it waterproof. Cover the base and sides of the
boat with pieces of sticky tape, to stop the
paper from getting soggy.

You could make a whole flotilla
of sampans using...

TURN TO PAGE 106 TO LEARN
HOW TO ADD SAILS TOO...

patterned paper

kitchen foil

newspaper

baking paper

91

SOLVE AN ENIGMA

Can you decipher the message on the Enigma machine below? Clue: check the switches on a machine the wires. Write the message and follow the wires. Write the message on a piece of paper as you decipher it.

NGB
Never Get Bored
Headquarters

*A CCCMEHU RSEKBEXME.MGEN HXEO !

TMO MR EAHTEMGNET LN SEO TTTHU TYECGLZVC.BE
RMEMR EFVCCCE, EH,C ESMEN HXESA OBE, LHGT E
SA E RVUOHELMX EVTETMELMOQCVLHS XYE

N QC.EFVSAESA ELMX EQANHT ER I NEU SE,MN XBE
TMEVEZRMFEVSJTE.MGY

HU RSED*

All double letters become triple letters **ON**

All words are written backwards **OFF**

All messages start and end with * **ON**

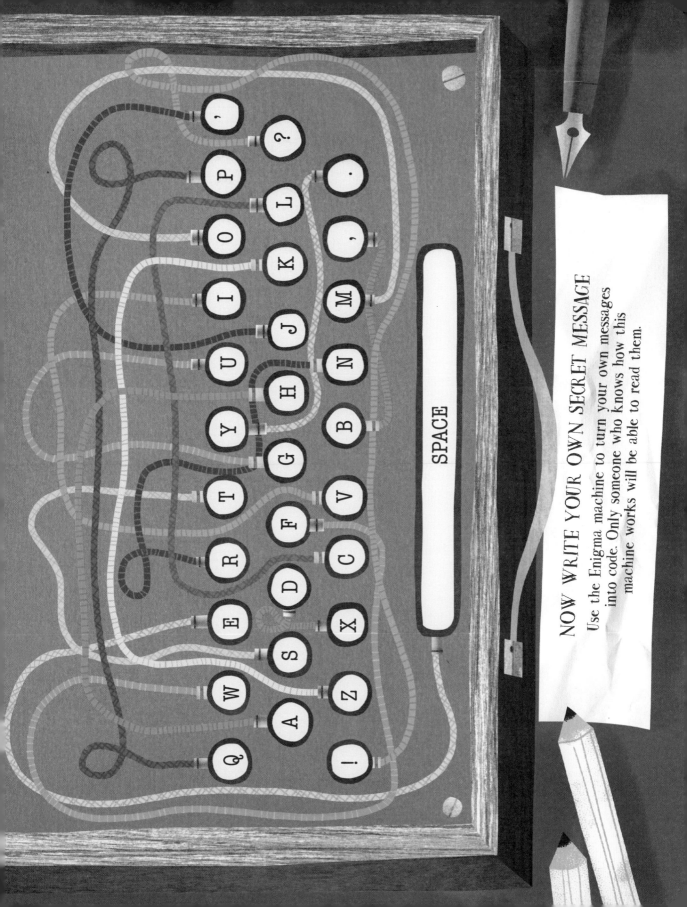

NOW WRITE YOUR OWN SECRET MESSAGE

Use the Enigma machine to turn your own messages into code. Only someone who knows how this machine works will be able to read them.

DRAW CATS...

Draw shapes with a crayon, and then use a black pen to fill in details.

Give your cat a tongue so it can lick its paw.

Draw a spiral, then add a face, ears and stripes.

Make lots of dashes with your pen for a long-haired cat.

Fill gaps between your drawings with pawprints and balls of yarn for cats to play with.

Shade in patches for a tabby cat.

Don't forget some claws.

Draw simple shapes before adding details: eyes, whiskers and noses.

...AND DOGS

Add movement lines for a wagging tail.

Draw an oval and two diagonal lines, then join them with a curve for a dog bowl.

Not all dogs look neat!

Doodle a poodle with squiggly lines for fur.

Draw a doghouse. Then, shade in parts, to make it look 3D.

Draw the outline of a dog, then scribble dots inside to make a dalmatian.

FLY A KITE

Build your own kite and send it soaring.

YOU'LL NEED:

scissors

tape

a thick plastic bag

3 fat drinking straws

a ball of strong string

a pen

a ruler

1

Cut the end of one straw on a slant. Insert this pointy end halfway inside another straw to make a longer straw.

2

Tie the long straw that you've made and a third straw together into a cross, like this.

3

Cut the bag open to make a large rectangular piece of plastic, and fold it in half.

4

Lay the cross along the fold. Using a pen and ruler, draw lines to connect the three ends of the straws. Cut along the lines.

5

Unfold the plastic and stick the four ends of the cross to the corners with enough tape, so they're well stuck. This is your kite sail.

You could decorate your kite by adding ribbons, if you like.

6

Now attach the ball of string to the kite sail. Thread the end of the string through the short straw and tie a knot to make a small loop.

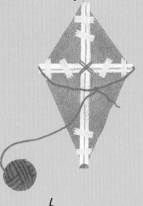

HOW TO FLY IT

First, unravel about 10m (30ft) of string.

WHEN? On a dry, windy day

WHERE? Away from trees, traffic and electric lines

Ask someone to hold the kite and let it go...

...while you run as fast as you can into the wind, tugging the string.

Once your kite is flying, unwind more string to let it go higher.

The first kites were made in China about 2,500 years ago.

In 1982, a team of kite flyers in America flew a kite continuously for 180 hours – that's over a week!

One of the largest kites ever flown was designed to look like the flag of Kuwait.

THE BOY WHO FLEW...

According to legend, long, long ago in Japan...

...Minamoto no Tametomo, a samurai warrior, was banished to an island with his son. His crime: disobeying the emperor.

You can't spend your life here.

Minamoto knew his son had to escape, but how? They began building an enormous kite...

Then one day, when the wind was just right...

...Minamoto tied his son to the kite and flew him all the way to the mainland.

PLAY AROUND THE CLOCK

This is a game to play on your own
with a deck of 52 playing cards.

JOKER

SETTING UP

Put any joker cards
aside, and shuffle
the deck.

*

Deal the deck into 13 piles
and arrange them into a
clock face like the one
on the right.

NOW... PLAY

Pick up the top card
from the pile in the
middle of the clock.

*

Tuck this card face up
under the pile that
matches its number.

*

Now pick up the top
card from that pile and
tuck it under whichever
pile it matches.

*

Keep playing until
you can't pick up any
more cards.

In this game, Ace
counts as 1, Jack counts
as 11, Queen counts as 12
and King counts as 13.

11   12   1

10   2

          13

9   3

8   4

7   6   5

JOKER

You finish the game
if you manage to turn all
the cards face up. If you
can't, shuffle the cards
and start again.

98

DO A CARD TRICK

You'll need a deck of cards and a willing volunteer.

PREPARE THE DECK

Shuffle the deck. Turn the bottom card so it's facing up. This is the trick card.

PERFORM THE TRICK

1

Hold out the cards in a fan shape. Make sure the trick card isn't showing. Ask a volunteer to pick a card.

2

Tell the volunteer to memorize their card, while you make the deck into a pile. Turn the whole deck over so the trick card is now on top.

Don't let anyone see you do this!

3

Take the volunteer's card back and slide it into the middle of the deck.

It must be facing down.

4

With your hands behind your back, turn up the trick card that's at the top of the deck. Then, turn the whole deck over.

Tell your volunteer you are using magic to reveal the card.

5

Now, spread the cards out on a flat surface. The volunteer's card will be face up.

Ta-da!

Practice makes perfect.

Yes, rehearse the trick a few times before you perform it.

MAKE MODELS

Cut out lots of circular pieces, then slot them together to make different models.

1
Use the bottom of a glass to draw lots of circles on a piece of cardboard. You'll need at least 30.

2
Cut out the circles. Then, cut four thin 'V' shapes into each one.

3
Slot the circles together like this.

Ideas for models:

How tall a tower can you build?

TOWERING AMBITIONS

Try building towers out of other things.

Cans

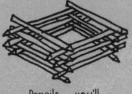

Pencils – you'll need two for each layer.

Playing cards

Lean pairs of cards together to make upside-down 'V' shapes, then balance flat cards on top.

The tallest tower of playing cards was built in 2007.

It was 7.87m (25ft, 9in) tall. Over 90,000 cards were used – but no glue or tape at all.

TURN SHAPES INTO PICTURES

The template (below right) is a tangram – a Chinese puzzle made up of different shapes that you can arrange to make pictures.

1. Put a piece of tracing paper or baking parchment over the template. Use a ruler and pencil to draw over the straight black lines.

2. Turn over the paper or parchment and put it over a piece of thick paper. Draw over the lines, pressing hard.

3. The pencil lines should now show on the thick paper. Cut out the different shapes following these lines.

You can now use your shapes to make these different pictures:

dog

house

goose

boat

rabbit

fox

cat

shark

1

2

3

Can you figure out how to make these three pictures too?

UNDERSTAND 'ELEPHANT'

Elephants use body language to 'talk' to each other.
Here are some of the things they can say...

What's that smell?

Trunk raised

Go away!

Ears spread wide

Hello

Wide mouth

High five!

Trunks twisted together

Let's go

Come and play

Trunk wrapped around tusks

Foot swung in direction of travel

Now try to speak 'elephant' too. Use your arm as a trunk.

Weighty facts

The African savanna elephant is the heaviest land animal. This is how it compares to some other mammals.

1

African savanna elephant

39 people

1,500,000 mice

1 tongue of a blue whale

Jumbo jokes

A trend for telling jokes about elephants started in the US in the 1960s.

A ridiculous question and a strangely sensible answer make up each joke.

Why do elephants paint their toenails red?
To hide in cherry trees

What time is it when an elephant sits on your bed?
Time to get a new bed

groan

Why do elephants have wrinkles on their ankles?
Because they tie their shoelaces too tight!

What do you call an elephant at the North Pole?
Lost

ho ho

ha ha

Can you make up your own elephant jokes?

Make an elephant
You'll need an empty plastic bottle with a handle.

1 Cut the top off a plastic bottle, around the bottom of the handle.

3 Trim the trunk, then add nails and eyes with a felt-tip marker.

2 Draw and cut out shapes from the front, back and sides to make four legs.

PLAY WORD GAMES

These three games will boost your word power while you play.

FILL THE GAPS!

You can play this game on your own.

Think of a word. Write its letters in a column.

Write the letters in the reverse order in a second column.

Write letters in the gaps to make new words. They can be any length.

```
S           E
A           G
UNDERSEA    A
S           S
A           U
G           A
ENDLESS
```

FAT CAT

– a game to play with several friends

1 Think of an adjective (a describing word) and a noun (a thing, person, place or idea) that rhyme with each other...

fat cat

2 Then, think of an adjective that has a similar meaning to 'fat' and another noun for 'cat'. Make sure these words don't rhyme.

chubby cheetah

3 Say these words aloud, challenging your friends to guess the original adjective and noun that rhyme.

THE ENORMOUS SANDWICH

– a game for two or more players

1 One player chooses the first thing to go in the sandwich and says...

I made a sandwich and in it I put... some salami.

2 The next player repeats what was said and adds something else.

I made a sandwich and in it I put... some salami and two pieces of cheese.

3 The game continues with players repeating and adding to the list.

I made a sandwich and in it I put... some salami, two pieces of cheese and sliced red onions.

4 If you forget something or say the wrong thing, you're out. The last person still playing is the winner.

104

CUT AND PASTE POETRY

In the 1920s, Romanian-French poet Tristan Tzara devised a new way of writing poems.
Follow these steps to copy his technique.

1

Cut out words from an old magazine or newspaper. You'll need at least twenty words.

2

Put the words in a bowl and stir them.

3

Pick out words one at a time, and arrange them on a piece of paper in the order you picked them.

HOW DOES IT SOUND?

happy GO to SUPERMARKETS

AT excited ing times

the YOU BARGAIN wants

dance MUSIC bananas s

A MONKEY is not just for HOLIDAYS

wait! for ME

You could write in extra words...

...or letters.

Or, switch some of the words around.

When you're satisfied with the order of words in your poem, glue it down.

SET SAIL

Make sails and a mast for a model boat, such as the origami sampan from pages 90-91.

You will need some paper, a pencil and a straw.

1 Cut three rectangles out of paper. They should be the same width as your model, but different heights.

2 Using the point of a pencil, make a hole at the top and bottom of each sail.

3 Thread a straw through the three sails, from biggest to smallest.

4 Stick a blob of poster tack in the middle of your boat and secure the mast in place.

Make a mast with two sails if you like.

Instead of the origami sampan, you could use an upturned shallow plastic container or lid for a boat.

TEST THE WATERS

Fill a tray with water and play these games with your boat.

OBSTACLE COURSE

Place a small stone in the middle of the tray. With a straw, blow the boat around the stone, trying not to touch it or the sides of the tray.

BLOW BY BLOW

Each player tries to blow the boat across the water to hit the opposite side. You score a point each time you manage to hit your opponent's side of the tray.

AROUND THE WORLD IN 1,082 DAYS

Between 1519 and 1522, Portuguese explorer Ferdinand Magellan's expedition became the first to sail around the world. Follow his journey on this map.

NORTH AMERICA

EUROPE

ASIA

The world really is round!

Day 585

Day 1
Day 1,082
Home at last!

N
W E
S

AFRICA

SOUTH AMERICA

This ocean looks calm. Let's call it the Pacific, which means peaceful.

AUSTRALASIA

Day 397
Crossing the Strait of Magellan*

Hurry home fast!

Day 973
No food left on board apart from rice

Magellan is killed by a poisoned arrow. Juan Sebastián Elcano is made captain.

*This narrow passage of water near the tip of South America connects the Atlantic and Pacific Oceans. It was named after Magellan's successful crossing.

BUILD A BEAST

Cut out pictures from old magazines, then put them together to make incredible new creatures. You could draw on patterns and extra body parts too.

RAAHHH

Does your creature have wings, fearsome claws or a tail?

Spots?

Paws?

A whale's tail?

Scales?

Spines?

Stripes?

When you're satisfied with your beast, glue it down on a piece of paper.

NOW TRY DRAWING ONE

Get together with two or more friends to draw monsters. Every person needs a piece of paper and a pen.

1 Draw a head at the top of your piece of paper. Then fold the paper down so only the bottom of the neck is visible.

Everyone passes their pieces of paper to someone else.

2 Now draw a body, making sure it's attached to the neck. Stop just above the legs.

Fold down the paper again, leaving the bottom of the body just visible before passing papers around again.

3 Add legs, flippers, tentacles or a tail to finish off the beast.

Fold again so your drawing is hidden, then pass on.

4 Unfold the papers to reveal your incredible creations!

THE LOCH NESS MONSTER

This Scottish monster was caught on camera in 1934...

...but 60 years later it was discovered that the photo actually showed a model head and neck, attached to a toy submarine.

MASTER SPYCRAFT

All good spies need several tricks up their sleeves, to keep their identities and messages secret.

DISGUISE YOUR VOICE

Keep who you are on the phone a mystery by changing your voice.

Try...

-pursing your lips.

-pinching your nose.

-pushing your tongue up against the roof of your mouth.

-doing an impression of someone.

-speaking with a slow drawl.

CHANGE YOUR LOOKS

Wear someone else's clothes.

Stuff a pillow inside your coat.

Rub hair product through your hair. Then comb in a very neat parting or ruffle it into a wild mane.

WALK LIKE ANOTHER

Study the way other people walk. Then try to copy their steps.

Try...

-taking short or long strides.

-bouncing on the soles of your feet.

-walking on your toes.

Remember, no one expects the unusual!

WHAT'S THIS?

It's a microdot. Spies hide messages in microdots because only their contacts who know to look at them through a microscope can read these words.

It's a microdot. Spies hide messages in microdots because only their contacts who know to look at them through a microscope can read these words.

It's a microdot. Spies hide messages in microdots because only their contacts who know to look at them through a microscope can read these words.

WRITE IN CODE
Dots & lines

Give your contacts this key. Tell them they can identify the letters by the lines around them and whether there is a dot.

= CAUTION

WRITE INVISIBLY

Use juice from a lemon for ink, and a toothpick for a pen. Keep dipping the toothpick in the juice as you write your message on white paper.

The words will only appear if you bake the paper in an oven at 150°C (300°F) for ten minutes.

Trio trick

First, split your message into groups of three letters.

CONTACT SPYMASTER HQ

CON TAC TSP YMA STE RHQ

Then, jumble each group of three letters by moving the first letter between the second and third.

OCN ATC STP MYA TSE HRQ

Psssst list

Hide words in lists. The number identifies the position of the letter in the decoy word next to it.

4 fish
2 beans
3 melons
1 potato   = HELP

Now try to decipher this message that uses three different codes...

EME ITN PGO NIT

5 socks
2 pants
1 fez
2 vests

SPY TIP

Using more than one code to write your message makes it especially hard to crack.

CONFIDENTIAL

BE INSPIRED BY A CLASSIC STORY

Around 100 years ago, Franz Kafka (1883–1924) wrote a story called 'The Metamorphosis'. It was about a man named Gregor who turned into a huge insect...

When Kafka read the story aloud to his friends, they all rolled around laughing.

SCENES FROM
THE METAMORPHOSIS*

*Metamorphosis is a word for when a thing – or person – turns into something else.

PRINT WITH VEGETABLES...

Cut up vegetables and dry them with a paper towel before brushing on paint and pressing them onto paper.

Use the top of a carrot or half a potato for different circles.

SPOTS AND DOTS

Print lots of spots on scrap paper to make your own wrapping paper.

You could use the end of a pencil to make smaller dots.

Print semi-circles with a quarter of a potato.

BEAUTIFUL BLOOMS

The base of a head of celery could make a rose.

NOW TRY PRINTING WITH...

- leaves you've found on the ground

- String you've tied into knots

- Coins

- Bubble wrap

WATERMELON

1 Paint a quarter of a potato with red paint and use it as a stamp.

2 When the red paint is dry, add black dots for seeds.

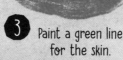
3 Paint a green line for the skin.

...OR YOUR FINGERS

Brush a thin layer of paint or ink onto an old sponge. Then, press your fingers on it and make prints.

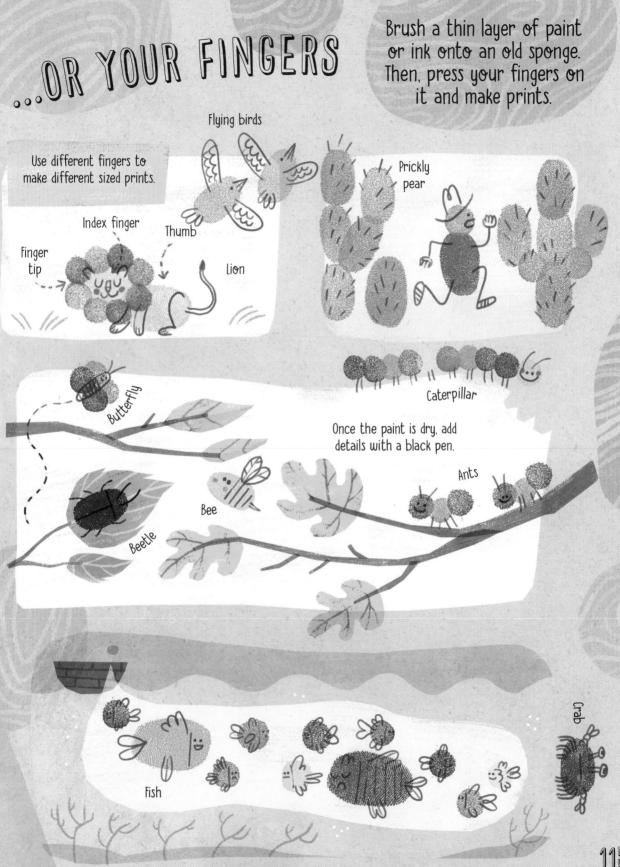

Use different fingers to make different sized prints.

Finger tip

Index finger

Thumb

Lion

Flying birds

Prickly pear

Butterfly

Caterpillar

Once the paint is dry, add details with a black pen.

Beetle

Bee

Ants

Fish

Crab

CRUNCH NUMBERS
Calculate a prediction

Think of a number lower than 20.

Now double it...

Add 10 to the answer.

Divide it by 2.

Now subtract the original number.

The answer should always be 5.

Now use this formula to impress your friends. Tell them that you're able to read people's minds before you begin.

Human stopwatch

Can you tell when a minute is up without looking at a clock?

Ask someone to time you, then count in your head and shout, 'Stop!' when you think 60 seconds have elapsed. It's harder than you think.

There are 1,440 minutes in a day...

...and 525,600 minutes in a year.

Open the safe

The five digit number needed to open this safe is hidden in a grid of letters. Starting at the orange circle, can you 'unwind' the snake of words that spells it out?

```
S U O H E S
A V E T Y V S
N I E T E D
D I F Y N N A
T H R T N D D
W O H U R E
```

Easy as pi?

If you divide the circumference of any circle by its diameter you always get this number:

3.14159265358979323846264338327950288419716939937510582097494459230781640628620899862803482534211706799...

circumference

diameter

This number goes on and on forever. It's named after the Greek letter pi, which looks like this: π

In 2006, Japanese mastermind Akira Haraguchi listed from memory over 100,000 digits of pi. Only the first 100 digits are listed above. How many can you memorize?

SPOT DIFFERENCES

Can you find 15 differences between these two scenes? Keep a list of the differences you spot.

LEARN BALLET POSITIONS

Try to stand in the five different positions that ballet dancers use to start and finish their dance steps.

First position

Put your heels together and turn out your feet.

Curve your arms as if you were holding a big beach ball.

Second position

Hold out your arms.

The space between your feet should be one and a half times your foot's length.

Third position

Arm curved in front

Arm out to the side

Put the heel of one foot against the middle of your other foot.

Fourth position

Arm curved above

Arm out to the side

Put the heel of one foot against the big toe of your other foot, then step forward with just your front foot.

Fifth position

Both arms curved above

Put the heel of one foot against the big toe of your other foot.

Now try a dance step...

This step is called a *pas de chat*, which means 'cat's step' in French.

Start in third position.

Lift your back foot.

Jump!

Land on the back foot.

Finish in third position.

Most ballet steps have French names because the first official ballet school was set up in France in the 17th century.

MAKE DECORATIONS

You can use plain paper, newspaper or old gift wrap to make these decorations.

Snowflake

Use a square piece of paper.

1 Fold the paper in half diagonally.

2 Fold in half again.

3 Fold the left and then the right side in along the dotted lines.

4 Trim off the pointed ends along the dotted line.

5 Snip off the tip of the triangle. Then cut out shapes on either side, like this, without cutting all the way across.

6 Unfold the snowflake.

You could turn the snowflake into a tutu for a

ballerina...

1 Fold a rectangular piece of paper in half lengthways.

2 Draw on a shape like this for your ballerina's body. Then cut along all the lines.

3 Unfold. Place the ballerina feet first through the middle of the 'snowflake' tutu.

You could thread a piece of string through the ballerina's arms to make a hanger.

Paper onion

Cut seven lengths of paper, like this:

x1
x2
x2
x2

Arrange the pairs of strips on both sides of the single shortest one in increasing size order, and staple them together like this...

Then, line up and staple the strips at the other end, too.

Staple or tape some ribbon at the top to hang each one.

TRAIN TO BE AN ASTRONAUT

Do you think that you have what it takes to go into space?

Most astronauts work on a flying science lab called the International Space Station (ISS).

Before you visit the ISS...

Get ready to wear a bulky suit

Put on thick gloves and try...

...using a knife and fork at lunch.

...writing with a pen.

...tying your shoelaces.

Prepare to float

Gravity is the invisible pulling force that stops us from floating away.

In space, people experience zero gravity, so they feel as if they're floating. Zero gravity can make astronauts feel queasy, too.

Riding a roller coaster is a good way to see if you have the stomach for zero gravity.

Keep fit and healthy

Astronauts don't use their bones or muscles much when they're floating in space, so they have to exercise every day to stay strong.

Lift up things above your head to strengthen your arm muscles.

Do 50 jumps making a star shape with your arms and legs.

5 0

You'll need to be able to read Russian too...

All astronauts fly to the ISS in a Russian spacecraft called a Soyuz. The labels on its controls are in Russian.

Russian is written in an alphabet, called Cyrillic.

RUSSIAN ALPHABET

Аа	*sounds like* **ar** in f**ar**	**Зз**	**z** in **z**ebra	
Бб	*sounds like* **b** in **b**ear	**Ии**	**ee** in m**ee**t	
		Йй	**y** in to**y**	
Вв	**v** in **v**oice	**Кк**	**k** in **k**ey	
Гг	**g** in **g**o	**Лл**	**l** in **l**and	
Дд	**d** in **d**ay	**Мм**	**m** in **m**oon	
Ее	**ye** in **ye**t	**Нн**	**n** in **n**ote	
Ёё	**yo** in **yo**lk	**Оо**	**o** in n**o**t	
Жж	**ss** in mi**ss**ion	**Пп**	**p** in **p**et	

Рр	**r** in **r**ock (make a rolled 'rrrr' sound if you can)
Сс	**s** in **s**un
Тт	**t** in **t**op
Уу	**oo** in sp**oo**n
Фф	**f** in **f**og
Хх	**ch** in Scottish word lo**ch**
Цц	**ts** in plane**ts**
Чч	**ch** in **Ch**arles

Шш	**sh** in **sh**irt
Щщ	**sh_ch** in fre**sh ch**eese
Ъъ	(silent)
Ыы	**i** in **i**ll
Ьь	(silent)
Ээ	**e** in **e**leven
Юю	**yoo**, like **yoo**
Яя	**y** in **y**ard

Can you work out how to say these Russian space words – and what they mean?

Астронавт

Союз

Планета

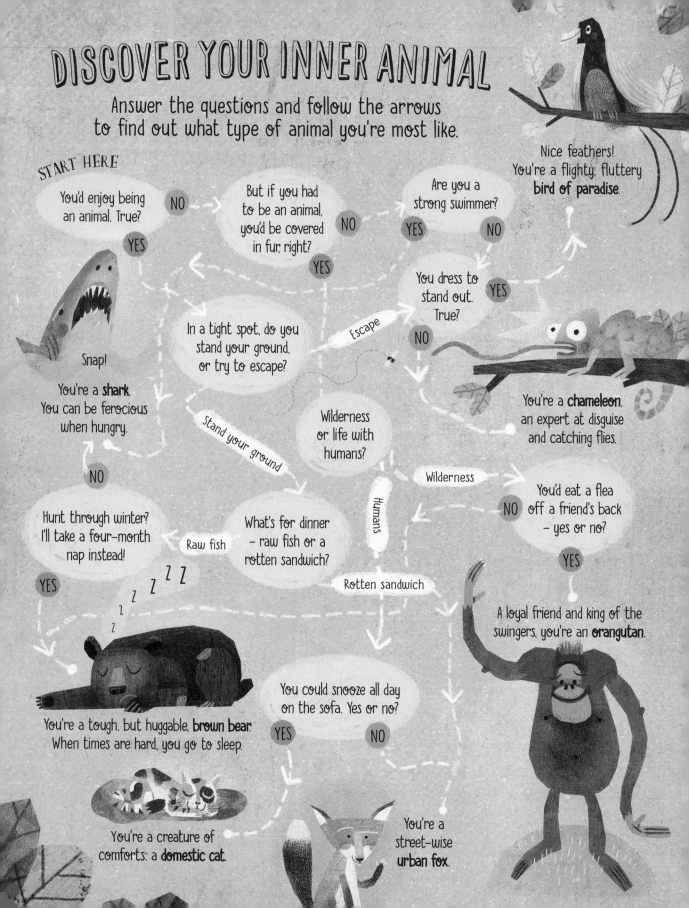

GO ON A SCAVENGER HUNT

All of these things can be found somewhere
in your Never Get Bored Book. Search through
the pages until you've spotted each one.

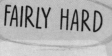 EASY

 FAIRLY HARD

HARD

FIENDISH

AND IF YOU'RE STILL BORED...

Dare to eat a teaspoon of mustard.

Start a dream diary. Write down your dreams when you wake up.

Balance a book on your head and try to walk without it falling off.

Have a tickle fight.

(Whoever laughs first, loses.)

Touch each of your teeth with your tongue. How many do you have?

Learn the 50 states of the USA in alphabetical order.

ALABAMA
ALASKA
ARIZONA
ARKANSAS
CALIFORNIA
COLORADO
CONNECTICUT
DELAWARE
FLORIDA
GEORGIA
HAWAII

IDAHO
ILLINOIS
INDIANA
IOWA
KANSAS
KENTUCKY
LOUISIANA
MAINE
MARYLAND
MASSACHUSETTS
MICHIGAN
MINNESOTA
MISSISSIPPI

MISSOURI
MONTANA
NEBRASKA
NEVADA
NEW HAMPSHIRE
NEW JERSEY
NEW MEXICO
NEW YORK
NORTH CAROLINA
NORTH DAKOTA
OHIO
OKLAHOMA
OREGON
PENNSYLVANIA

RHODE ISLAND
SOUTH CAROLINA
SOUTH DAKOTA
TENNESSEE
TEXAS
UTAH
VERMONT
VIRGINIA
WASHINGTON
WEST VIRGINIA
WISCONSIN
WYOMING

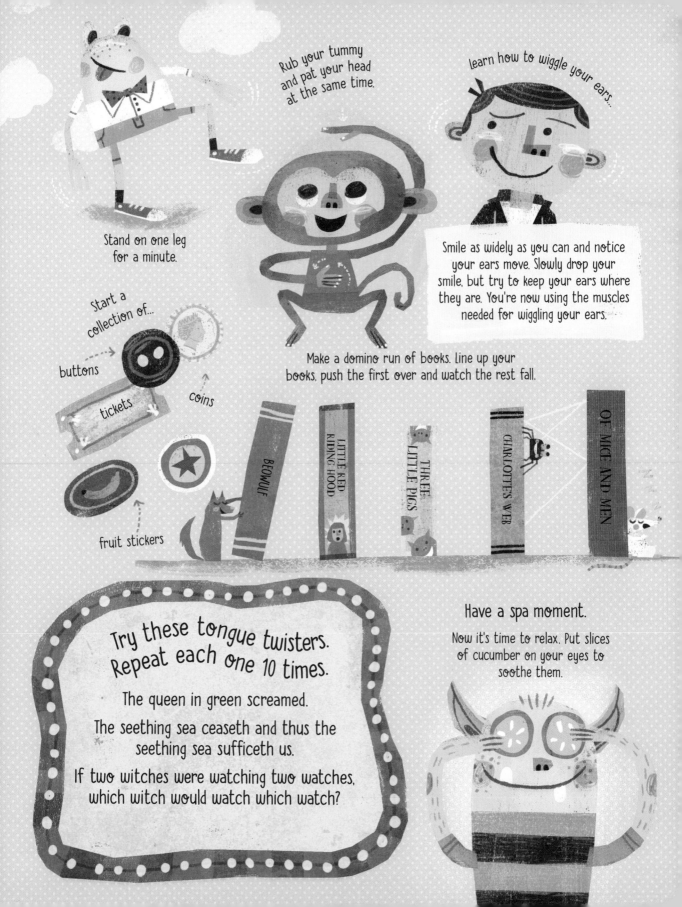

Rub your tummy and pat your head at the same time.

learn how to wiggle your ears...

Stand on one leg for a minute.

Smile as widely as you can and notice your ears move. Slowly drop your smile, but try to keep your ears where they are. You're now using the muscles needed for wiggling your ears.

Start a collection of...

buttons

tickets

coins

fruit stickers

Make a domino run of books. Line up your books, push the first over and watch the rest fall.

BEOWULF

LITTLE RED RIDING HOOD

THREE LITTLE PIGS

CHARLOTTE'S WEB

OF MICE AND MEN

Try these tongue twisters. Repeat each one 10 times.

The queen in green screamed.

The seething sea ceaseth and thus the seething sea sufficeth us.

If two witches were watching two watches, which witch would watch which watch?

Have a spa moment.

Now it's time to relax. Put slices of cucumber on your eyes to soothe them.

CHECK YOUR ANSWERS

2–3 BORED, HUH?

I'M SO VERY BORED: dry, yes, boor, redo, robe, some, void, berry, sever, sieve, sorry, remove...

8–9 TEST YOUR SENSES

SPOT IT:

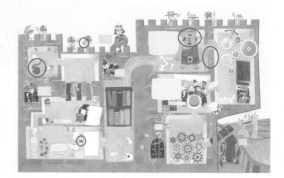

18–19 STRETCH YOUR BRAIN

BIRD'S EYE VIEW: (from left to right) someone frying an egg, two people with umbrellas and puddles, someone playing golf and a pirate on an island

TURN AROUND: Move the line, shown in red, in the direction of the arrow, then rotate the page so it is landscape.

CONUNDRUM: Your right hand

AFTER SHOT: A snowman melted away.

RIDDLES OF THE SPHINX: 1. Someone riding an elephant 2. An envelope 3. lunch and dinner

26–27 BECOME A PASTA COGNOSCENTE

PASTA PUZZLES: Tangles A, C and D make knots. Verona, Chieti and Palermo are Italian cities.

30–31 SURVIVE IN THE JUNGLE

DINNER TIME:
A. Longhorn beetle grub
B. Agave weevil
C. Giant silkworm caterpillar
D. Nightcrawler worm
E. Bush cricket
F. Robber fly
G. Armadillo woodlouse

34–35 MASTER PHOTO TRICKS

SURPRISING CLOSE-UPS: 1. Soap bubble 2. Frogspawn
3. A type of broccoli called Romanesco

38–39 SOLVE MYSTERIES

PROBLEM POISONING: The poison was in Lord Livingstone's straw. Lady Lavinia drank straight from her glass.

THE VANISHING VANDAL: The vandal fired a bullet made of ice through the window. It broke the vase, and then melted.

WHODUNNIT?: Cuthbert Chase stole the racehorse. He shaved his beard and tried to sell his blonde wig (see Classifieds) before he was arrested.

GETAWAY CAR GETS AWAY: Vehicle CL23 was the getaway car. The thieves changed it to EU28 with strips of tape.

46–47 ESCAPE FROM THE CASTLE

- The turquoise path is safe.
- Potion ingredients are circled in red:

- It will take 56 minutes to do the dishes.
- The book titles are all written backwards. The second book from the right on the second shelf reads: PUSH BOOK TO OPEN PASSAGE.
- The answer to Olf's question is Friday.
- Turn the lever to the left.
- You could cut the cake like this.
- The wheel on the right of the middle row is the only one with an uneven number of handles.

51 BUILD A SNOWMAN

SNOWY WORDS: snowed, snowdrift, snowdrifts, snowflake, snowflakes, snowstorm, snowball, snowballed, snowfall, snowman, snowmen, snowboard, snowdrop, snowdrops, snowshoe

SNOWY FACTS: Not every snowflake is unique. In 1988, a scientist spotted two identical snowflakes under a microscope. They were from a storm in Wisconsin, USA.

52–53 WRITE ABOUT A QUEST

WHICH BOOK?: 1. *The Wizard of Oz* 2. *Alice's Adventures in Wonderland* 3. *The Lord of the Rings*

56–57 DECODE HIEROGLYPHS

60 FIND WORDS

bug, gut, gem, rot, lid, toe, fig, fir, nit, tin, sum, mud, the, tow, sit, can, vote, more, some, dill, mint, bare, toys, sure, slur, soil, doll, city, toll, site, pave, germ, prey, vary, boil, vapid, night, bidet, cumin, hello, cages, juice, broke, slice, slurp, slide, singe, modem, quote, bored, silver, willow, sluice, slider, relish, cudgel, remove, motive

62 TEST YOUR MEMORY (PART 2)

Invisa is the superhero that's missing.

76–77 QUESTION EVERYTHING

1. a 2. b 3. a 4. True (The Eiffel tower was the tallest structure in the world until the Chrysler Building in New York was built in 1928.) 5. b 6. a 7. True (Rattlesnakes are deaf.) 8. True (Newborn babies have 270 bones, which join together so adults have 206 bones.) 9. c 10. b 11. b 12. a (Rhinos follow their ears more than their eyes.) 13. c 14. c 15. a 16. b 17. b 18. b 19. False 20. c 21. c 22. False (Tim Berners-Lee invented the World Wide Web.) 23. Neptune 24. b 25. c 26. b (This is because they contain lots of Vitamin C.) 27. a 28. b 29. c 30. b

80–81 CUT A SILHOUETTE

SILHOUETTE SPOTTING: 2 beards, 3 ponytails, 6 glasses. There are more glasses.

83 PLAY RING TOSS

RING CHALLENGE:

85 BE A DINOSAUR DETECTIVE

A. Triceratops B. Parasaurolophus C. Styracosaurus D. Allosaurus E. Tyrannosaurus

92–93 SOLVE AN ENIGMA

The coded message between the asterisks says: HELLO AGENT Z, DO YOU READ ME? SOMEONE HAS OUR SECRET MESSAGES. LUCKILY, NO ONE WILL BE ABLE TO READ THEM, BECAUSE THE ENIGMA CODE IS SO COMPLICATED. REPLY WITH THE CODE PHRASE NEVER GET BORED, SO I KNOW IT'S YOU. AGENT X

101 TURN SHAPES INTO PICTURES

116 CRUNCH NUMBERS

OPEN THE SAFE: Thirty-five thousand two hundred and seven

117 SPOT DIFFERENCES

Changes made to the right-hand scene are circled in red:

120–121 TRAIN TO BE AN ASTRONAUT

Астронавт means astronaut. Союз is how Soyuz is written in Russian. Планета means planet.

123 GO ON A SCAVENGER HUNT

Moon (p67), Queen (p99), Ballerina (p118), Cup (p52), Robot (p116), Lion (p18), Saxophonist (p81), Whale (p102), Boat (p91), Vase (p38), Skull (p47), Roller coaster car (p120), Eagle (p124), House (p37), Photographer (p35), Cello (p23), Star (p33), Newspaper (p41), leaves (p65), Cap (p76)

GO ONLINE

The internet is brimming with fun things to do, but they're hidden among lots of boring stuff. For links to only the best online activities, go to the Usborne Quicklinks website at www.usborne.com/quicklinks and type in the keywords: 'Never Get Bored'.

You'll find links to websites where you can...

Watch a volcano erupt

Discover how tigers 'talk'

Write your own computer programs

And meet some robots

Please follow the internet safety guidelines at the Usborne Quicklinks website.

The websites recommended at Usborne Quicklinks are regularly reviewed but Usborne Publishing is not responsible and does not accept liability for the availability or content of any website other than its own, or for any exposure to harmful, offensive or inaccurate material which may appear on the internet.

Additional writing by
Rose Hall and Megan Cullis

Edited by Jane Chisholm

Additional design by
Jamie Ball

Photographs on pages 35, 59 and 108 © thinkstock